THE SEVEN KEYS TO COMMUNICATING IN BRAZIL

THE

7

KEYS TO

COMMUNICATING

IN

BRAZIL

An Intercultural Approach

ORLANDO R. KELM

DAVID A. VICTOR

Georgetown University Press | Washington, DC

Library of Congress Cataloging-in-Publication Data
Names: Kelm, Orlando R., 1957– author. | Victor, David A., 1956– author.
Title: The seven keys to communicating in Brazil : an intercultural approach/Orlando R. Kelm and David A. Victor.
Description: Washington, DC : Georgetown University Press, 2016. | Includes bibliographical references and index.
Identifiers: LCCN 2015048675 (print) | LCCN 2015050430 (ebook) | ISBN 9781626163522 (pb : alk. paper) | ISBN 9781626163515 (hc : alk. paper) | ISBN 9781626163539 (eb)
Subjects: LCSH: Business etiquette—Brazil. | Business communication—Brazil. | Corporate culture—Brazil. | Intercultural communication—Brazil. | Communication and culture—Brazil. | National characteristics, Brazilian. | Americans—Employment—Brazil.
Classification: LCC HF5389.3.B7 K45 2016 (print) | LCC HF5389.3.B7 (ebook) | DDC 395.5/20981—dc23
LC record available at http://lccn.loc.gov/2015048675

18 17   9 8 7 6 5 4 3 2   First printing

Printed in the United States of America

Text design by click! Publishing Services
Cover design by Connie Gabbert Design + Illustration.
Cover photo is of a mural in honor of the architect Oscar Niemeyer by artist Eduardo Kobra, courtesy of the Associated Press (André Stefano / Fotoarena).

For my wife Tonia, and my three children,
Tamara, Devin, and Michael.

—ORLANDO R. KELM

For my wife Dianne, and my three daughters,
Megan, Constance, and Danielle.

—DAVID A. VICTOR

CONTENTS

FIGURES AND TABLES

PHOTOGRAPHS

PHOTOGRAPHS

As part of the case study in chapter 8 of this book, you will read the story of Carolina Battipaglia, the Latin American marketing director for ABC Security Systems. She tells a fascinating story of the cultural conflicts that come up in her job while trying to balance company global objectives with local applications. We would like to thank Carolina for her gracious interview and the telling of her story. The problem is, of course, that in order to protect the privacy of individuals, we changed the names of the people, the company, and the location of the events. Still, "Carolina," you know who you are, and thank you for such insightful observations about your professional world.

At the same time, we openly recognize the excellent analysis of the cultural experts who commented on the case and who gave their recommendations from North American and Brazilian perspectives: Christine Uber Grosse, chief executive of SeaHarp Learning Solutions; Mary Risner, associate director of the Center for Latin American Studies at the University of Florida; Stephen Kaufmann, founder and chief executive of LingQ .com; Denise Coronha Lima, founder of Rio Total Consultancy; Gleverton Munno, senior manager of external relations for the Global Operations Team at Dell; and Wagner Palmiere, senior manager of the US Central Region, Mexico, and Central America at Ascendant Technology.

One of the keys to intercultural competency is the ability to listen, to adapt, to be flexible, and to be open to new ideas. It is not a mere coincidence that these same qualities describe those at Georgetown University Press, especially Hope LeGro, who assisted us in making this book more applicable to a wider readership.

And, of course, to all our Brazilian friends and colleagues, thank you for providing us with nearly four decades of experiences in your homes, your schools, your companies, your churches, and your personal lives.

A few years ago the Johnny Walker liquor company created a spectacular commercial titled "Keep Walking." In the video, the rocks and mountains in Rio de Janeiro were transformed into a giant who was finally waking up. The reference, of course, was to Brazil, the sleeping giant whose moment had finally arrived. Those who follow Brazil will also remember the cover photo on *The Economist* in 2009, which depicted Rio's Christ the Redeemer statue as a rocket, with a caption reading "Brazil takes off." But then in 2013 *The Economist* followed up with another cover photo of the Christ the Redeemer rocket, this time crashing and falling out of the sky, with the caption reading "Has Brazil blown it?"

And so it is that on the world stage, Brazil both appears and disappears. At times, Brazil seems to be on the cusp, ready to take a prominent position as a world leader, the "B" in the BRIC group of large, fast-growing countries—Brazil, Russia, India, and China. And then, all of a sudden, it feels like two steps forward, one step back. Still, in economic, corporate, geopolitical, and cultural terms, Brazil has major importance. And despite notable setbacks, Brazil's importance has indisputably grown significantly during the past thirty years. What is clear, considering the current economic and political challenges that Brazil faces, recovery and growth will take longer and require more care than what many suspected.

This importance is especially evident for North America, where Brazil's emergence has mattered immensely in both trade and higher education. Brazil is the United States' seventh-largest trading partner. Likewise, the United States is Brazil's second-largest trading partner (having been edged out in 2013 by China). Brazil is Canada's eleventh-largest trading partner, and this relationship is growing rapidly, having jumped in size by 25 percent from 2007 to 2012 alone. With respect to higher education and study abroad, Brazil has jumped from almost being off the radar to the fifteenth-largest destination for US students. Moreover, since the beginning of the Ciência sem Fronteiras (Science without Borders) initiatives in 2011, Brazil has committed to sending 100,000 Brazilians to study abroad, with two of their top three destinations being universities in the United States, which is ranked number one among country destinations, with 26,300 in the first three years; and Canada, ranked number three, with 7,000 (the United Kingdom was ranked second, with 9,500).

THE LESCANT APPROACH: HOW TO READ THIS BOOK

Given the importance of Brazil, and its position in international operations, the purpose of this book is to provide a guide for North Americans on how to conduct business and otherwise interact culturally with Brazilians. To give structure and focus to our analysis, we follow what we call the "LESCANT approach." LESCANT is a simple acronym that represents seven areas where intercultural communication may differ from one group of people to another:

- *L*anguage,
- *E*nvironment and technology,
- *S*ocial organization,
- *C*ontexting,
- *A*uthority conception,
- *N*onverbal behavior, and
- *T*ime conception.

Based on this approach, the first seven chapters of this book follow the seven categories of LESCANT.

Chapter 1 deals with issues related to the "L" of LESCANT: language. Perhaps no other element of international business is so often noted as a barrier to effective communication across cultures as differences in language. Brazilians speak Portuguese, a language that few North Americans know. There is an important give and take in communication that relates to translation, interpretation, the nonnative use of another's language, the borrowing of terms from another language, and a host of other issues related to what happens when we cross linguistic lines.

In chapter 2 we deal with issues related to the "E" of LESCANT: the environment and technology. Our physical environment both communicates key points within our culture and changes our thinking and behavior in many ways. Consider, for example, transportation and climate. Aside from Alaska, virtually nowhere is as sparsely inhabited as the Brazilian Interior or the Canadian Far North. There is virtually nowhere in the continental United States that is unreachable by road, even in the emptiest stretches of Wyoming. By contrast, *most* of the land areas of Brazil and Canada are unreachable by road (and, for all practical purpose, even by other means). In chapter 2 we also touch on several other areas of the environment, such as the size of a person's office, the use of air-conditioning, and population density. There are simply thousands of ways in which the nature of our physical surroundings differs from one culture to another.

Chapter 3 deals with issues related to the "S" of LESCANT: social organization. We can define social organization broadly as the common institutions and collective activities that members of a culture share. These include such areas as family, religion, education, sports, community organizations, the role of women in society, and how we use our leisure time. The influence of these institutions and collective activities shapes the behavior of people in all aspects of life, from business to education to raising our families. Many of the variables that we examine in this book happen without our being aware of them. In the case of social organization, we may be aware of the differences but often are not aware of the implications. Perhaps because these differences are overt, it is sometimes easy for us to be condemnatory or critical when others deviate from our own system of social organization. For example, the concept of sexual harassment exists in both Brazil and North America, but Brazil has almost none of the same concepts behind the laws regarding what people in both

Canada and the United States call a "hostile work environment." The concepts behind them are simply foreign in Brazil, a fact made all the more problematic by legal action that results from what Brazilians (men and women alike) view as perfectly innocent behavior. These are the sorts of issues that are addressed in this chapter.

Chapter 4 deals with issues related to the "C" of LESCANT: contexting. Although we minimize the use of technical terminology in this book, in the case of "contexting," there is simply no good equivalent. The great cultural researcher Edward T. Hall coined the term to describe how much of what one says or writes is understood directly or implicitly through understanding the context for the communication.

In high-context communication, we depend more on gathering information that we share in common, which then does not need to be specifically stated because it is understood. But in low-context communication, we depend more on actual words or gestures, so we need to state them specifically. On the contexting scale, North American culture is among the lowest in the world, but Brazil is among the countries at the high end.

In high-context cultures like Brazil, people rely on stored information. This means that Brazilians have (or need to have) considerable knowledge and experience in common before they can communicate effectively with each other. Because Brazilians store more information (i.e., gather more context) than North Americans, they choose not to put into words things that they assume are obvious. In high-context interactions, people have stored information that they all share. As a result, in high-context cultures people can usually anticipate what is not specifically stated.

The opposite is true of communication in low-context cultures such as the United States and Canada. Because speakers store less information, knowledge, and common experience, their communication depends more on the actual words. In low-context cultures, most things need to be stated explicitly—there is very little reading between the lines. From a Brazilian perspective, North Americans sometimes overstate the obvious. The implications of all this are explored in chapter 4.

The "A" of LESCANT is covered in chapter 5, which deals with issues related to how Brazilians and North Americans divergently view authority and power. The two cultures also have differences in who has (or, at least, is seen as supposed to have) power. Brazilians and North Americans also differ in how that power is shared or exchanged. Authority conception deals with how we view our boss, and how we view those who report to us and to our peers. This affects both how decisions are made and how we show status.

Authority conception also affects things such as how we trust (or, in the case of the United States, *distrust*) authority figures. It also plays into how governments operate and the role of politics at all levels, from the head of state to office politics. This brings up all sorts of interesting things when dealing with Brazil, because Brazilians need to create informal, unofficial networks of authority to get things done. The Brazilian *malandro* is something that has no direct equivalent in North America, but it is the Brazilian way of creating enough informal authority to get things done in the absence of official power and authority. All this is summed up in the special term *jeitinho* for this Brazilian way of doing things.

Chapter 6 deals with issues related to the "N" of LESCANT: nonverbal behavior. We all know that we convey our meaning by more than just the words we use. How we move, how we dress, and how far apart we stand when we talk all contribute to what we mean to communicate. The interpretation of non-verbal messages grows problematic in cross-cultural situations, because the chances of misinterpretation increase when people from different societies attempt to communicate. A harmless or friendly gesture in one culture may be understood as threatening or antagonistic in another.

Our nonverbal communication also includes eye contact, gestures, touching, our sense of personal space, dress and adornment, and how we respond to colors, smells, and symbols. No two cultures share the same nonverbal communication style, and there are variations even within the same culture. Brazilians often comment that North Americans are cold, aloof, or "stand-offish." But how often is this perception simply a misinterpretation of nonverbal behavior?

The final piece of the LESCANT approach deals with the concept of time, which is considered in chapter 7. Although we often think of time as something very real and measurable, we seldom consider the cultural nuances related to our concept of time. To take an example from another country, in Bahasa Indonesia people use the excellent term *jam karet* (rubber time) to explain the Indonesian concept of time. Thus, in Indonesia, time stretches like rubber when pressure is applied to it. This notion of rubber time is also a pretty good way of explaining how time is seen in Brazil. However, it would be inaccurate to think that people in these countries have no sense of time; they do—but in these countries, time is affected by personal relationships. When personal relationships affect specific situations, time stretches to accommodate them.

Conversely, in the "time is money" countries, personal relationships are subordinated to the clock or calendar. It is not that people in these countries have no sense of personal relationships; they do—but for them, keeping to a schedule takes precedence over personal relationships. This is a subtle but very important point. Our view of time is tied to how we approach our personal relationships, and our view of personal relationships is equally tied to our view of time. These are two sides of the same coin—with Brazil on one side and North America on the other.

In chapter 8 we provide readers with a cultural vignette, a cultural case study—a story based on actual Brazilian–US interactions in a workplace setting (with the names changed). The issues that come up in the case study exemplify many of the topics that we present in the book, and readers may apply the LESCANT approach to their own analysis of what these problems might be.

Following the case itself, we have provided the opinions of executives from both the United States and Brazil regarding what they found significant in the scenario. These executives give their own views, providing another level of understanding of US–Brazilian realities. Finally, after the executive commentary, we provide a section with questions and topics to help the reader assess this case's cultural issues and to develop recommendations about solutions.

Readers will notice that most chapters in this book include a large number of photographs. Our approach to using photos is simple. Every time we notice something that seems culturally out of sync, or different, or somehow gives us a sense that something is not quite right, we try to identify how this might fit into the LESCANT approach. Is the problem related to a language issue? Do these differences stem from how we perceive authority? Do we have unique ways of looking at time? The use of photographs gives us practice in observing these cultural issues. And by identifying the categories, we begin to assess our cultural uniqueness. The photographs in this book are designed to sharpen our ability to observe and assess these cultural differences. We illustrate many of these changing variables with photographic support, and we hope they will be as valuable as the written explanations we provide.

THE TERM "NORTH AMERICAN"

As we begin, it is important to address the term "North American." Many Brazilians (in fact, many Latin Americans in general) feel that the term "American" applies to the entire Western Hemisphere, from Hudson Bay in the Arctic to Tierra del Fuego at the Antarctic-facing tip of South America. From this perspective, Brazilians are as much "Americans" as people from the United States. When people from the United States refer to themselves as Americans, referring only to their nationality, it raises problems in this regard. The Brazilian press generally uses the adjective *norte-americano* for people or things from the United States. The problem here, however, is that North America may also refer to Canada and Mexico as well as the United States. Although many (though not all) Mexicans recognize that *norte-americano* does not include Mexico (Mexicans themselves use the unhyphenated Spanish equivalent *norteamericano*), the "North American" designation does become more complicated in the Canadian context. Canadians, unlike Mexicans, *do* view themselves as "North Americans." Using the term *norte-americano* (or its English or Spanish counterparts) to refer only to the United States therefore poses as much of a problem for many Canadians as using the word *American* does for many Latin Americans. We simply advise readers that when Brazilians say *norte-americano*, they are referring exclusively to people from the United States.

Although we do not have a specific answer to this terminology quandary, we realize that most of what we share in this book about Brazil corresponds well to standard communication within the United States and Canada (and especially Anglophone Canada). This is not to suggest that the United States and Canada are culturally identical—far from it! Yet most of the topics in this book that culturally divide Brazil from the United States by and large represent the same cultural divides between Brazil and Canada. Where this is not the case (e.g., for the issues of the environment and technology, authority conception, and nonverbal behavior), we expand the cross-cultural comparison from a two-sided to a three-sided discussion. Unless otherwise noted in this way, however, we use the term "North American" here to refer to both the United States and Canada. It is our hope that by sidestepping the "North American" terminology issue, we have expanded the usefulness of this book for US and Canadian readers alike.

And with that, let us begin our look at the aspects of intercultural communication with Brazilians. We have been interacting with Brazilians for more than thirty-five years, and it is a pleasure to share the insights we have gleaned along the way. Our hope is that these insights, within the context of the LESCANT approach, will serve to give you a better understanding of the beauty of the not-so-sleepy giant, the "B" in the BRIC.

BRAZILIAN

Language

That's a Lot of Portuguese!

Perhaps there is no more central issue for intercultural communication than the choice of language. Even in situations where two parties are totally bilingual, a decision will still need to be made about which language is going to be used. In most situations, at some level, someone needs to make a concession to use a language in which he or she is less fluent. In other situations when even this partial fluency is absent, we are forced to resort to interpreters and translators. So it is appropriate that we begin by looking at language. It is inevitable that the use of one's native language or the use of a local language will drastically affect intercultural communication.

In this chapter we give a brief introduction to the use and role of Portuguese in Brazil, and a short description of the use of English as a lingua franca. We then look at a number of examples to see how English loanwords are used in Brazil. The chapter ends with a few recommendations for how to deal with language differences between native speakers of English and Portuguese.

When we look at Brazil and consider how language becomes an issue of intercultural communication, the first thing we note is that Brazil is the only country in Latin America where Portuguese is the official language of the people. This is not an insignificant feature. Portuguese is the seventh most common language in the world. Only Mandarin, English, Spanish, Hindi-Urdu, Arabic, and Bengali have more speakers than Portuguese. There are more speakers of Portuguese than there are of Russian, Japanese, German, French, Korean, and Italian, just to name a few. Unfortunately, many uninformed people simply assume that Brazil is a Spanish-speaking country—which, by the way, drives Brazilians crazy.

According to statistics from the US Central Intelligence Agency's *World Factbook*, Brazil's population of 201 million represents more than half the population of South America.[1] No other country even comes close. The second-most-populated country in South America is Colombia, which at 45.7 million has less than a quarter of Brazil's population. Even when we compare South America with North America, Brazil has almost twice the population of Mexico (116 million) and more than five and a half times the population of Canada (34.7 million).

Brazil is the only Portuguese-speaking country in Latin America, in part because of a semi-unexpected result of the 1494 Treaty of Tordesillas. At that time, to resolve land disputes between the world powers Spain and Portugal, a line was drawn along the meridian that was about 370 leagues west of Cape Verde in West Africa. This was designed to give the lands west of that line to Spain (mainly the Americas) and those east of that line to Portugal (mainly Africa and the coasts toward India). It turns out, however, that part of Brazil actually extends farther east than what people had supposed. As a result, Portugal claimed part of "their" land in the Americas, when Pedro Álvares Cabral landed in Brazil in 1500. Five hundred years later, the result is that Brazil, with its historical roots in Portugal, is now the only Portuguese-speaking country in the Americas.

Portuguese is a Latin-based language, and thus it is similar, at least to some degree, to the other so-called Romance languages (e.g., Catalan, French, Italian, Romanian, and Spanish). This similarity is especially important in the case of Spanish, because Brazil is almost completely surrounded by Spanish-speaking countries. In fact, native speakers of Portuguese almost automatically understand quite a bit of Spanish. The inverse is less true, however. Native speakers of Spanish may get the gist of basic Portuguese, but they actually understand it much less than the other way around. This leads at times to perceived slights, for some Brazilians seem to feel that Spanish speakers are intentionally unwilling to understand what is being said. Brazilians who are more acquainted with their Spanish-speaking counterparts, however, recognize this for what it is: Comprehension is more difficult going from Spanish to Portuguese than vice versa.

To give a brief example, let us look at the words for various body parts and the numbers from one to ten in Spanish and Portuguese:

Portuguese: *cabeça, braço, perna, pé, mão, olhos, nariz, boca, orelhas*

Spanish: *cabeza, brazo, pierna, pie, mano, ojos, nariz, boca, orejas*

Portuguese: *um, dois, três, quarto, cinco, seis, sete, oito, nove, dez*

Spanish: *uno, dos, tres, cuatro, cinco, seis, siete, ocho, nueve, diez*

We see that many of the words look similar. However, in actual speech, many of the Portuguese words are shorter than their Spanish equivalents. And Portuguese has many more contractions than Spanish. As a result, when hearing Spanish, Portuguese speakers catch most everything that is said; but when hearing Portuguese, Spanish speakers seem to feel that something is missing. Here is a simple example to illustrate this concept:

Portuguese: *No livro da escola tem a foto da lua.*
Spanish: *En el libro de la escuela, tiene la foto de la luna.*
English: In the book from the school, there is a picture of
the moon.

Indeed, the Portuguese words are shorter, and there are more contractions. Imagine being a speaker of Spanish who hears *da lua* for *de la luna* (of the moon). It just sounds like parts are missing. Conversely, a Brazilian who is used to hearing *da lua* gets additional parts when hearing the Spanish *de la luna*.

WHAT BRAZILIANS THINK OF NONNATIVE PORTUGUESE SPEAKERS

When a person goes to Brazil to work professionally, the Brazilians will not necessarily expect that person to speak Portuguese, but they will be pleasantly surprised if he or she does. At the same time, it is becoming more common to find foreigners who do speak Portuguese. Additionally, and not ideally, as long as you do not suppose that Spanish is the language of Brazil, Brazilians are also open to communicating with foreigners with a little mix of English, Portuguese, and Spanish.

Brazilians are quite receptive to people who try to speak Portuguese, even if they speak the language poorly. This type of response is not a given. For example, in the United States, in general terms, people are simply assumed to speak English. If foreigners do not speak English well enough to be readily understood, many Americans become frustrated and give up trying to communicate at all, sometimes even equating an inability to speak English with a lack of intelligence. This is not the case in Brazil. Someone who does not speak Portuguese well is viewed simply as someone who lacks skill in the language. It is not a given that every foreigner will speak Portuguese.

Some countries tend to emphasize more than others the need to speak a language correctly in terms of grammar. For example, much of French identity is wrapped up in the French language. Although most French businesspeople will tolerate the usage of grammatically weak French, there is a stronger resistance to this than, say, the usage of grammatically weak French in Quebec or grammatically weak English in the United States. Brazilians tend to fall into the category of accepting limited control of Portuguese more readily.

Additionally, speaking Portuguese imbues the foreigner who is trying to use the language with an added benefit. Brazil may be the language of more than 200 million people, but it is not a widespread second language. In fact, only an estimated 30 million people speak Portuguese as a non–mother tongue. By contrast, among the 338 million speakers of French, only 80 million or so speak it as a mother tongue; and of the 1.5 billion people who speak English, only 330 million or so speak it as their first language. Moreover, of the 220 million people who call Portuguese their mother tongue, more than 90 percent live in Brazil. As a result, when someone chooses to learn Portuguese, most Brazilians presume that this is because he or she has a sincere interest in Brazil, and that led to his or her decision to study Portuguese in the first place. This is seen as a compliment, and is likely to predispose Brazilians favorably to the foreigner who is speaking (or even just trying to speak) Portuguese.

BRAZIL AND THE PORTUGUESE-SPEAKING WORLD

As the world's largest Portuguese-speaking nation in both population and economic terms, Brazil has a somewhat special relationship with other Portuguese-speaking nations. There are nine nations where Portuguese is the official language: Brazil, Angola, Cape Verde, East Timor, Equatorial Guinea, Guinea-Bissau, Mozambique, Portugal, and São Tomé and Príncipe (figure 1.1).

In 1996 Brazil and six others among these nations (East Timor and Equatorial Guinea joined later) formed the Comunidade dos Países de Língua Portuguesa, specifically to further political, cultural, and economic cooperation among fellow Portuguese-speaking countries. Because Brazil dominates these other countries in size and economic clout, the result has been

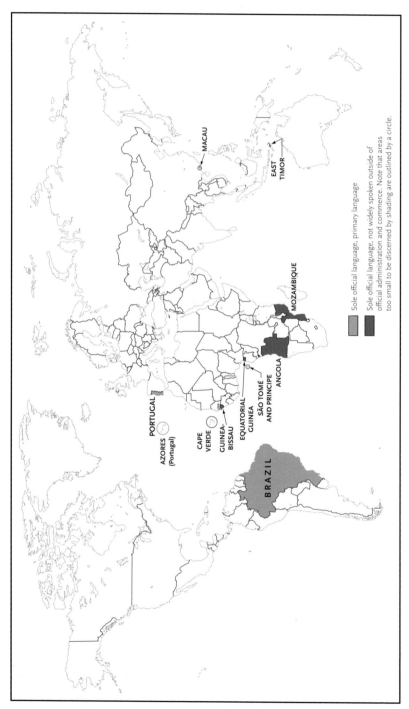

Figure 1.1
The Portuguese-Speaking World

MACAU

EAST TIMOR

MOZAMBIQUE

PORTUGAL

AZORES (Portugal)

CAPE VERDE

GUINEA-BISSAU

EQUATORIAL GUINEA

SÃO TOMÉ AND PRINCIPE

ANGOLA

B R A Z I L

Sole official language, primary language

Sole official language, not widely spoken outside of official administration and commerce. Note that areas too small to be discerned by shading are outlined by a circle.

much stronger trade ties with these countries, especially those in Africa. Currently, Brazil's third-largest African trade partner is Angola, and its fourth-largest is Mozambique. Brazil also enjoys a number of political and cultural exchanges with its African neighbors. In chapter 3 we expand on this situation a bit further.

HOW MUCH ENGLISH IS USED IN BRAZIL?

It is undeniably true that worldwide, in many ways, English is the lingua franca for professional activities. It is also true that many Brazilians do speak at least some English. And it is also the case that if you are only dealing with highly educated, high-level upper management, perhaps you will find yourself being able to use English in Brazil. However, the use of English in Brazil breaks down quickly. If a person plans on dealing with suppliers, factory workers, local civic leaders, secretaries, and just about any other sector, expect your ability to use English to be more limited.

For example, if a foreign visitor goes to major museums, historical sites, or other typical tourist locations abroad, it is quite common to see English translations on many of the written descriptions. This is less common in Brazil. When going to restaurants abroad, one frequently sees English translations of the menus. This is less common in Brazil. When travelers go to hotels, take a taxi, or use public transportation services like a subway, in many countries there will be a fairly strong presence of English-language options. This is less common in Brazil. Even in São Paulo and Rio de Janeiro, there is less provided in English than what is often seen in comparable major cities in other countries of the world, including major cities in South America, such as Santiago, Lima, and Buenos Aires. In second-tier cities—such as Salvador, Curitiba, and Belo Horizonte—the presence of anything in English is even less likely.

According to Education First, which publishes an English Proficiency Index, poor English is one of the key competitive weaknesses of Latin America. Brazil ranks forty-first out of the sixty countries that appear on the index.[2] The index divides countries into five major levels of English proficiency: very high (e.g., Sweden, Norway, and the Netherlands); high (e.g., Poland, Germany, and Portugal); moderate (e.g., Argentina, the Czech Republic, South Korea, and Ukraine); low (e.g., Brazil, Turkey, and Iran); and very low (e.g., Algeria, Thailand, and Libya). The index also ranks a number of other countries in Latin America. Brazil actually ranks lower than such countries as China, Russia, and Vietnam. To be fair, Brazil does rank higher than many Latin American countries, but it is still far down on the low scale.

English-language learning in Brazil is similar, in many ways, to the learning of Spanish in the United States. English is required in most Brazilian schools, although it is often taught by teachers who themselves are not fluent in English, and often with the goal of passing tests without emphasis on comprehension or conversation. That is to say, almost every Brazilian can say that they studied some English in high school, or that they took a couple of years of English in college. Similar to North Americans who study Spanish, however, it is easier to say how long one studied a language than it is to actually use the language. Most Brazilians are just as confident in their use of English as North Americans are in their use of their high school Spanish.

HOW ENGLISH IS USED IN BRAZIL

Although Brazilians generally have a low proficiency in English, there is actually a strong presence of English in loanwords— which, however, are often modified for local pronunciation and usage. For example, Santhier, a Brazilian company that produces paper products, has a napkin with the brand name "Snob." Chances are that they were trying to create the image of a member of high society, a connoisseur of fine foods, or an expert in a given area. Clearly, however, they did not intend any of the nuances of the English word "snob" that hint at being condescending, overbearing, or disdainful.

There is also a shoe store on Avenida Paulista in São Paulo named "Fatty Man." One wonders how the logic of choosing such a name came about. In the United States we sometimes

1.1 Snob Napkins
Ah yes, Snob napkins for those with refined tastes.

1.2 Fatty Man Store
And you can wear "Fatty Man" shoes too!

hear that "sittin' fat" has a positive connotation that refers to living the good life. Still, it is a stretch to think that "Fatty Man" was chosen with that idea in mind. It is even more difficult to imagine how the store's name relates to shoes at all.

As foreign words are adopted by other cultures, there is often an interesting transition in their meaning. For example, in Brazil the word *outdoor* means billboard. Because all the advertising billboards are indeed outdoors, it is not surprising that somehow Brazilians modified the meaning of *outdoor* to represent that actual billboard, and not just the advertising sign. By association, Brazilians also have a word, *busdoor*, which refers to advertising that is posted on city buses. If *outdoor* is an advertisement that is along the street, then *busdoor* can easily be an advertisement that is on a bus. Native speakers of English simply will not understand the meaning of *busdoor*, and to be fair, many Brazilians will not either. Frequently in Brazil, young boys make deliveries all over town by riding their motorcycles in and out of traffic. One

1.3 Busdoor Advertising
The *busdoor*, where advertising is on the side of a bus.

1.4 Let's Lanches
Drop in for a snack at Let's Lanches.

of these workers is called a *motoboy*. Again, by association, there can also be a *motogirl*. Brazilians thus invent a creative array of words that began from English-language words but have a new connotation that no native speaker would understand.

Other words also change in meaning. For example, the English word "lunch" is written *lanche* in Portuguese. However, *lanche* really takes on the meaning "snack," which can be a light meal at any time, frequently in the late afternoon. The actual word for "lunch" in Portuguese is *almoço*, which carries all the cultural connotations of the way that Brazilians eat their main meal in the middle of the day. We know of a Brazilian family that moved to the United States and enrolled their daughter in elementary school. The poor girl heard about "lunch" and thought it was time to get out her snack, only to find out that the teacher told her it was not lunchtime. It took a while for them to figure

1.5 "Tommy" Cerveja
This is where "Tommy" means *tome*, "to drink." Put it together, and you've got "drink *cachaça* (similar to rum)."

out what the misunderstanding was all about. In Maricá, just outside Rio de Janeiro, there is a small restaurant named "Let's Lanches," a beautiful combination of English and Portuguese language borrowing.

There are other examples of extremely interesting wordplays that happen because of language shifts. In photo 1.5, we see a clever example of T-shirts that were made to imitate Tommy Hilfiger's red-and-white logo. The play on words here is that the name "Tommy," when pronounced in Portuguese, sounds like the verb *tome*, which means "take" or "drink." As such, *tommy cachaça* means "drink rum." This is actually a fairly sophisticated twist in meanings and sounds, which can only be appreciated with a knowledge of both English and Portuguese.

A number of years ago, we saw a small restaurant in Belo Horizonte named São Duíche. Turns out that the word "sandwich" in Portuguese, *sanduíche*, is borrowed from English. However, "san" sounds a lot like the Portuguese word *são* (saint), as in São Paulo, São Caetano, and São Vicente. The restaurant's clever owners took the word *sanduíche* and changed it to "Saint Duíche"—that is, São Duíche. Only a speaker of Portuguese will truly understand the play on words, but it was an extremely creative example

1.6 Pringooools
Scoring a "goal" with "Pringoals" potato chips.

of a word that was borrowed from English. In 2014, when the World Cup was held in Brazil, Pringles Potato Chips created an imaginative carton where the name "Pringles" was changed to Pringooools. Ah, if only the host nation could have scored a few more goals during that competition. For our purposes, once again we witness the interesting interplay in the blending of English loanwords with typical Portuguese pronunciations.

When talking about hot dogs in Portuguese, the direct translation and the most common way to say it is *cachorro quente*, literally *cachorro* (dog) and *quente* (hot). However, Brazilians sometimes use the borrowed "hot dog," which is pronounced something like "hochee dogee." In photo 1.7, the street vendor not only sells hot dogs but also sells hamburgers; but the sign says *x-tudo*. A *x-tudo* is a cheeseburger with everything on it. The letter "x" in Portuguese is pronounced "shees," which sounds similar to the English word for "cheese." Even though the Portuguese word for "cheese" is *queijo*, when referring to hamburgers,

1.7 Hot Dog e X-Tudo
A "hochee dogee" and a "cheese-everything," please.

Brazilians will often use the letter "x" as an abbreviation for "cheese." As a result, a *x-tudo* is a "cheese-everything," meaning a hamburger with cheese and everything else on it too.

Where things really get difficult for speakers of English is to learn how Brazilians pronounce the loanwords that come from English. The *outdoor* mentioned above is pronounced something like "ouchy-door," and *lanche* comes out something like "luhn-she." In general, relatively few words in Portuguese end in a consonant, so Brazilians naturally add a vowel sound to the end of many loanwords. As a result, one hears such things as "pingy-pongy" for ping pong; "kingy-kongy" for King Kong; "Vicky-vapo-ruby" for Vicks Vapor Rub; "down-lowgee" for download; and "fay-see-bookie" for Facebook. There are hundreds of such examples. Sometimes Brazilian pronunciations of loanwords imitate the spelling, and other times they imitate the original English sounds. As a result, for example, Citibank is pronounced something like "see-chi-bang-key." This is close to the English pronunciation of "bank," even though Portuguese has its own word, *banco*, with a completely different pronunciation. Conversely, the word for AIDS in Portuguese is pronounced "ay-gees," which follows the Brazilian pronunciation for all words spelled with "ai." It is difficult to predict when a loanword will have a pronunciation based on spelling and when it will have a pronunciation based on the sounds.

SUGGESTIONS ABOUT LANGUAGE TO ENCOURAGE GOOD COMMUNICATION

Given the issues discussed above, we offer the following recommendations, as related to language issues in cross-cultural communication with Brazilians:

General Strategies

You can do several things to facilitate understanding for Brazilians. To begin, Brazilians will not understand many of the idiomatic and slang expressions that native speakers of English use every day. For example, avoid references to sports that may be unknown to Brazilians. For example, expressions like "getting to first base," "striking out," and "hitting a home run" are less understood by people who are not familiar with baseball. Without knowing it, many times North Americans use phrases from pop culture in ways that nonnative speakers cannot follow. References to events, stories, phrases, and clichés from classic TV series are often difficult for Brazilians to follow. Imagine, for example, how hard it is to relate to references to "no soup for you" if you are unaware of *Seinfeld*.

Second, slow down! As native speakers, we do not realize how fast we speak. A Brazilian is expecting to hear, for example, "What are you going to do today?" but instead she hears "Wacha gunna dudaday?" We help them out by speaking a little slower, rephrasing our sentences with new words, and keeping our vocabulary simple. If our interaction with Brazilians is mainly in the form of presentations, be sure to use written support. Many times Brazilians can read English better than they can understand it orally. It helps to have a written outline and visual examples of oral presentations.

When we find ourselves listening to Brazilians who are speaking English to us, there are also a few things that will help in understanding them. First, in Portuguese there is a tendency to drop pronouns. Consequently, many Brazilians also drop their pronouns when speaking English. For example, Brazilians tend to say "I like" instead of "I like it" or "I buy" instead of "I buy it." Once we are aware of this, we will hear it a lot. Second, native speakers of English almost always answer questions with the word "do"—for example, "Do you eat bananas? Yes, I do." In Portuguese, however, Brazilians answer questions with the same verb as in the question. They say, in essence, "Do you eat bananas? I eat, yes." Do not be surprised when Brazilians also follow this pattern when they are speaking English to you.

Third, Brazilians pronounce words that start with an "r" with a sound that is more like an "h." As a result, for example, the word "river" sounds like *hiver*, and the word "rush" sounds like *hush*. This takes some getting used to. But now you know why Rio sounds like *hio* and Ronaldo sounds like *honaldo*. Fourth, the letter "t" in Portuguese often sounds like "chee." Notice that if Brazilians talk about "cheamwork," they are referring to teamwork. Similarly, the letter "d" often sounds like "gee." What this means is that when you have a "deal," you will hear a Brazilian say that you have a *geal*.

Conversely, if you are learning Portuguese, there are a few things to be aware of as you speak with Brazilians. First, native English speakers answer questions with a direct "yes." Brazilians, however, almost never answer a question with a direct yes. Instead, they answer with a verb—as noted above. When nonnative speakers answer questions by saying "yes" (*sim*), it often comes across as sounding very blunt and overemotional. To a Brazilian ear, nonnative speakers often sound angry when they are not, or overly excited when they are not. "Do you want some bananas? YES! Should we prepare the contract? YES! Do you like the food? YES!" Be aware that what Brazilians normally do is to answer the question with the main verb, and then they can add "yes" for emphasis: *quero, sim* (I want, yes); *preparamos, sim* (we prepare, yes); and *gosto, sim* (I like, yes).

A second recommendation for those who are learning to speak Portuguese is to soften your speech by avoiding the simple present tense. That is to say, avoid saying directly things like *Eu quero falar com João* (I want to talk to João) or *Você pode falar com João?* (Can you talk to João?). Instead, Brazilians soften their sentence by putting the verb in a past or conditional tense: *Eu queria falar com João* (I wanted to talk with João), or *Você poderia falar com João?* (Would you be able to talk to João?) This will sound much more polite, but it is a tendency for new learners of Portuguese to simply use the present tense.

Knowing That the Language We Use Is Tied to Emotions

It is good to remember that we all have a sense of linguistic ethnocentrism. Whether for historical or political reasons, we all feel more comfortable in expressing ourselves in our native language. This is partly because there is an emotional connection between our words and our feelings. For example, if a man is speaking his native language, if he says out loud to a woman, "I love you," there will be an emotional feeling that goes with that declaration. The man will feel the impact of that phrase, and the woman will feel the power of those words. She may blush, she may smile, she may think that the man is naive, but she will feel the emotion of the phrase. This is not true when we speak in a foreign language. When speaking a foreign language, we can often say words and phrases, but we do so without the emotions that are connected. If that same man, for example, were to use his nonnative Portuguese to say *Eu te amo* to a Brazilian woman, he could do so without any of the attached emotional feelings. The problem, however, is that if he said those words to a Brazilian woman, she would hear them with all the emotion that goes with it. (It is precisely for this reason that people often think it is fun to learn swear words in another language. We can repeat them without the same emotional connection.) Be careful, however, because often our words sound extremely harsh, blunt, direct, and bold when speaking a foreign language.

This works both ways. When Brazilians use English with native speakers of English, sometimes they will sound more blunt than they mean to. Similarly, when nonnative speakers of Portuguese use Portuguese with Brazilians, they will also sound more blunt that they mean to. We have seen countless examples where misunderstandings arise because listeners misinterpret the emotions of statements that are made by nonnative speakers of a language. For example, when North Americans speak Portuguese, if they use English intonation patterns, they come across to Brazilians as if they were more emotionally charged that they really are. Do not be surprised when Brazilians ask you to calm down, when all along you think you are being calm. And from the other end, do not be surprised if Brazilians sound overly happy, nice, and supportive when speaking English.

In a similar way, be aware of how much, as native speakers of a language, we can subtly change our speech. If we want to sound a little more formal, show a little more respect, or indicate a little more seriousness, we can do so with minute changes in our language. Notice, for example, the subtle difference in phrases like "I want to talk to you," "I would like to talk to you," "I was hoping to talk to you," and "If you have a moment, I was wondering if I might talk to you." When we are using English with our Brazilian counterpart, we bring all this subtlety into our communication. This happens practically subconsciously. It may very well be, however, that our Brazilian counterpart is limited to much less flexibility. Be aware of these limitations, and give the nonnative speaker a break. If you are learning Portuguese, you will feel the same limitations in reverse. You may witness the most beautiful sunset over Corcovado, one that inspires you to believe that God created the world for the joy and pleasure of humankind. However, with your limited Portuguese, you will look at your Brazilian friend and simply say *bonito* (pretty).

Becoming a Brazilian Insider

We often hear how speaking a language allows one to be considered a member of a group. Clearly, a person who can speak Portuguese in Brazil will be able to participate in conversations, read public postings, and understand details about Brazilian society in ways that are not available to those who do not speak the language. Two examples will suffice. Brazilians often tell people that there is no translation for the word *saudade*. North Americans may think that it means nostalgia, longing, yearning, homesickness, or missing something. It does not matter what translation you give to *saudade*; a Brazilian will always retort that it means much more than any of the translations that you give it. And indeed, it is true. Brazilians connect with *saudade* in a way that is only understood when one becomes familiar with the language and culture. In the second example, Brazilians are famous for what is called *jeitinho*. *Jeitinho* refers to the finagling, contriving, and bending of rules. It refers to the way that people get around procedures and rules in order to work around things. In all sincerity, Brazilians do not have a unique ability to work around rules. They simply have the best word to describe it. (*Jeitinho* is considered further in chapter 5.)

If you are going to work with Brazilians for any length of time, try to learn to speak at least some Portuguese. The insights to Brazilian thought that come from an understanding of their language are simply not available to those who never learn the language. We are not naive enough to believe that all business interactions will happen in Portuguese. However, even if your Portuguese language skills are used more in informal and non-work-related contexts, you will be rewarded with new insights into Brazilian behavior.

Learn a Few Phrases in Portuguese
If you are unable to learn Portuguese with true fluency, then it always helps to at least learn a few words, phrases, and social niceties. Here are some words that even first-time travelers who go to Brazil can easily learn:

Oi	Hello
Tchau	Goodbye
Tudo bem?	Is all well?
Tudo bem.	All is well.
Sim	Yes
Não	No
Prazer	It is a pleasure
Por favor	Please
Obrigado	Thank you—*spoken by a man*
Obrigada	Thank you—*spoken by a woman*

Bom dia	Good morning
Boa tarde	Good afternoon
Boa noite	Good evening; good night
É	It is, yea

USING WHAT YOU KNOW ABOUT LANGUAGE TO ENCOURAGE GOOD COMMUNICATION

Of all the LESCANT categories, perhaps language is the most obvious, because it directly affects our ability to communicate verbally. Still, by being aware of the LESCANT approach, we put ourselves in a stronger position to observe intercultural communication issues that are placed before us. Because language is the most obvious category, it is also the one where we can make the most direct adjustments in our communication with others, including those from Brazil.

SUMMARY OF BRAZILIAN LANGUAGE

What we know about Brazil's language:

- There are more than 200 million native speakers of Portuguese in Brazil.
- Portuguese is the world's seventh most common language.
- Portuguese is a romance language, similar to Spanish and Italian.
- Most Brazilians understand a lot of Spanish.
- Spanish speakers do not understand much Portuguese.
- There is little expectation that foreigners can speak Portuguese.
- Brazilians appreciate any nonnative attempt to speak Portuguese.
- Very few Brazilians actually speak fluent English.
- Relatively few signs and English-language translations are available in Brazil.
- In Brazil there are many English-language borrowings, with unique pronunciation.

Communication strategies when using English with Brazilians:

- Recognize that someone makes a sacrifice to use their nonnative language.
- Avoid idiomatic and slang expressions from pop culture.
- Avoid American sports metaphors.
- Slow down and repeat yourself.
- Reinforce communication with written visuals.

- Recognize that our North American style of communication comes across as blunt, direct, and bold.
- Realize that Brazilians drop pronouns when talking in English.
- Brazilians pronounce "r" like an "h" (river = "hiver").
- Brazilians pronounce "t" like "chee" (teamwork = cheemwork).
- Recognize that native speakers feel the emotion of words.

Communication strategies when using Portuguese with Brazilians:

- A few key phrases and social niceties go a long way.
- Answer with the verb, not *sim* (yes) or *não* (no).
- Soften speech by avoiding simple present tense.

2

BRAZILIAN
Environment

What a Huge Country!

Looking at the environment allows us to focus on the physical things around us that may be culturally specific. Our environment can be the types of chairs we sit in and the lighting of the room, or it can be our natural physical surroundings, like mountains, rivers, altitude, and weather. All the physical things that surround us are aspects of our environment.

It is interesting to examine the environment when talking about good communication. Unlike language, which is hard to ignore, we often fail to notice all the different physical things, even though we are surrounded by them. We are less aware of physical things that are culturally identifiable. For example, if a person has only walked on carpeted floors in apartments, it is easy to not even be aware of the fact that not every apartment has carpeted floors. When we begin to be exposed to other cultures, there are thousands of things that we notice for the first time, simply because we have never known anything different. The object of this chapter is to help you identify some of these types of things as related to Brazil, and to help you become more observant about these potential environmental differences.

Although categories tend to overlap, it is useful here to look at seven factors related to the environment that have an impact on professional activities in Brazil. In this chapter we discuss each of these as it relates to Brazil:

1. Topography and country size;
2. Population size and density;
3. Wealth, gross domestic product (GDP), and per capita income;
4. Crime and safety issues;
5. The climate and the weather;
6. Architecture, buildings, and office space; and
7. Environmental responsibility.

TOPOGRAPHY AND COUNTRY SIZE

Brazil is huge geographically. In fact, it is the fifth-largest country in the world in land area. It is slightly larger than the size of the continental United States (figure 2.1).

Brazil is by far the largest country in South America; it is more than three times the size of Argentina, the continent's next-largest country. In European terms, Brazil is almost twenty-four times the size of Germany. In fact, Germany would fit almost exactly into Mato Grosso do Sul, which is only Brazil's sixth-largest state. As with other giant countries (e.g., Russia, Canada, the United States, China, and Australia), the concept of distance is much different in Brazil than in smaller countries. Brazilians think little of traveling distances for a business trip that would be intimidating by European or Japanese standards.

Like the United States and Canada, Brazil is so large that it has multiple time zones. We should keep in mind that though this is something that these three countries have in common, in world terms, this is actually quite unusual; most countries have only one zone. Additionally, Brazil's internal time zone differences are a bit more complicated, because only some parts of

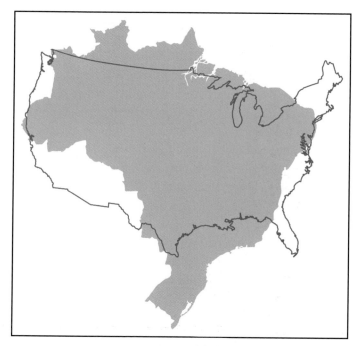

Figure 2.1
The Geographic Size of Brazil Relative to That of the United States

Brazil change to Daylight Savings Time. During Standard Time, Brazil has four time zones.

Because Brazil constitutes such a large landmass, its terrain and climate vary widely. Some parts are located above the equator, and some extend below the Tropic of Capricorn. The Northeast of Brazil is famous for its tremendous droughts in the *caatinga* semideserts, while the Pantanal region in Mato Grosso contains the world's largest wetlands. Much of Brazil is covered by thick forests, red soil, and green vegetation. Brazil has been called the "lungs of the world." The country has huge forests— it has been estimated that 20 percent of the world's oxygen is produced in the Amazon rain forest alone. Similarly, 20 percent of the world's total water flow comes from the Amazon River.

Although not the world's longest river (that distinction belongs to the Nile), the Amazon is in fact the world's largest flow of water, covering the world's largest river drainage basin.

Not only does it have more water flow than the next seven largest rivers combined but, in practical terms, the Amazon also provides Brazil with a nearly unlimited source of freshwater and a powerful and inexpensive means of shipping goods to the sea (but going upriver against the flow is quite a different matter). The Amazon, however, also has less positive features. Every year, the Amazon floods, roughly tripling the amount of land surface it covers. The resulting "flooded forests" (called *várzea* forests) prevent any substantive development of the land for commercial use. Also, because the Amazon rain forest is so important to the world in ecological terms, Brazil faces considerable pressure not to develop much of the region. Although many Brazilians support efforts to protect the Amazon River Basin from development efforts, many other Brazilians have expressed resentment of the attendant foreign critics of their efforts to develop the basin, indicating that they are unduly keeping Brazil from reaching its full potential. This is a particularly sensitive issue when the criticism is leveled by European countries such as Germany and the United Kingdom, which long ago cut down many of their own original forests.

In the interior of São Paulo State, there are miles and miles of sugarcane plantations, whereas in Porto Alegre one finds land suitable to vineyards. In the same way that the majestic topography of the Grand Canyon does not represent what the whole of the United States looks like, the Amazon does not represent what Brazil looks like. This is especially the case because Brazilians identify with their regional origins and their regional ways of life. This is not simply because of ethnic diversity and historical origins, but also because of the country's sheer distances and distinctive features.

Brazil is simply a country that cannot be summarized by one single physical look. Foreigners who work in Brazil and who work with Brazilians will gain favor when they appreciate this fact. Part of this is due to the physical peculiarities of each region of the country. Yet Brazilian regionalism's effect on the culture is much more marked than that of, say, the United States, which is similarly diverse in its physical characteristics.

Not only is Brazil very large geographically; it is also very large in terms of population. Let us begin with a brief look at some of the implications of Brazil's population and population density. Brazil is not only the world's fifth-largest country in size but is also the fifth-largest country in population, at 201 million. In terms of business potential, this places Brazil firmly in the category of market population giant (along with China, India, Indonesia, and the United States). That said, Brazil's population is nowhere near as evenly distributed as those of the other four population giants. In fact, the vast majority of Brazil's 201 million people live within 200 miles of the coast (figure 2.2).

This lopsided distribution of population makes for some unusual characteristics within the Brazilian marketplace. For instance, Brazil's population density ranks 169th (with only 62 people per square mile). By comparison, the United States has 75 percent greater density than Brazil (and the United States is considered a country with a low population density). As for the other population giants, Indonesia has more than five times the population density of Brazil, China has almost six times, and India has more than fifteen times.

Conversely, the coastal areas of Brazil are extremely densely populated. The State of São Paulo, for example, has a population density of 468 people per square mile. Even more revealing, according to city mayors, Greater São Paulo (São Paulo and its surrounding municipalities) ranks as the world's twenty-fifth most densely populated city, with 23,880 people per square mile.[1] Other Brazilian cities in the top fifty rank as follows: Recife, thirty-first (20,940 people per square mile); Rio de Janeiro, thirty-fifth (17,819); and Porto Alegre, forty-ninth (12,486). By comparison, Los Angeles is the most densely populated city in the United States, ranking only ninetieth (7,154).

According to statistics from the Instituto Brasileiro de Geografia e Estatística, seventeen cities in Brazil have a population of more than 1 million.[2] By contrast, the United States has only ten cities of more than 1 million, and the entire European

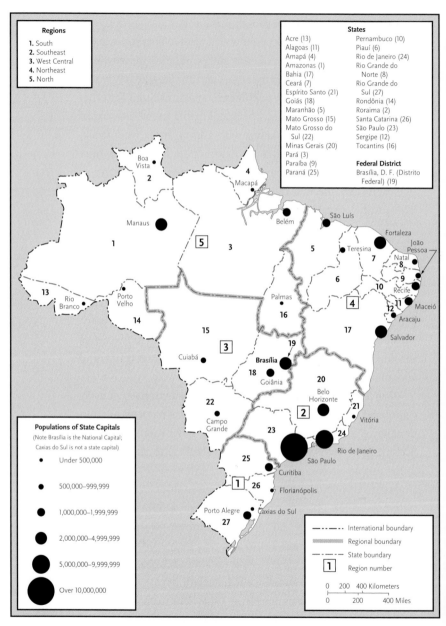

Regions
1. South
2. Southeast
3. West Central
4. Northeast
5. North

States

Acre (13)
Alagoas (11)
Amapá (4)
Amazonas (1)
Bahia (17)
Ceará (7)
Espírito Santo (21)
Goiás (18)
Maranhão (5)
Mato Grosso (15)
Mato Grosso do Sul (22)
Minas Gerais (20)
Pará (3)
Paraíba (9)
Paraná (25)

Pernambuco (10)
Piauí (6)
Rio de Janeiro (24)
Rio Grande do Norte (8)
Rio Grande do Sul (27)
Rondônia (14)
Roraima (2)
Santa Catarina (26)
São Paulo (23)
Sergipe (12)
Tocantins (16)

Federal District
Brasília, D. F. (Distrito Federal) (19)

Populations of State Capitals
(Note Brasília is the National Capital;
Caxias do Sul is not a state capital)

• Under 500,000

• 500,000–999,999

● 1,000,000–1,999,999

● 2,000,000–4,999,999

● 5,000,000–9,999,999

● Over 10,000,000

–··–··– International boundary

▓▓▓ Regional boundary

–·–·– State boundary

1 Region number

0   200   400 Kilometers
0   200   400 Miles

Figure 2.2
Brazil's Urban Population Distribution
Source: World Bank data.

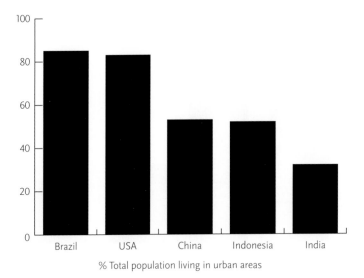

Figure 2.3
Brazil's Urban Population Compared with the Other Population Giants
Source: World Bank data.

Union has only fifteen cities over 1 million.[3] Moreover, all of Brazil's million-plus cities, except for Manaus and Brasília, are located within that 200-mile-wide strip along the coastline.

Another useful business statistic is the percentage of a country's population that is urban. The more urbanized a country's population, the easier it is for businesses to reach that country's market potential. The urban population of Brazil is 168,602,145, which is about 85 percent of the total number of citizens. In this regard, Brazil is the most urbanized of the five population giants (figure 2.3).

WEALTH, GDP, AND PER CAPITA INCOME

Brazil also looks very promising among the population giants with respect to its growing affluence relative to China, India, and Indonesia. When GDP per capita is measured by purchasing power parity (PPP, which is per capita income adjusted for differences in currency valuation and the price of most goods), Brazil

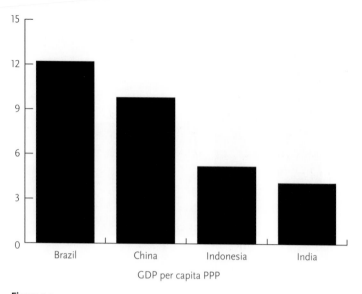

Figure 2.4
Brazil's GDP Per Capita (PPP) Compared with the Other Population Giants
Source: World Bank data.

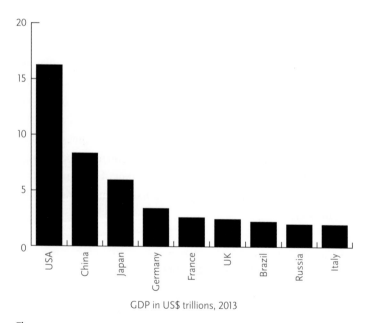

Figure 2.5
The Size of Brazil's Economy Compared with Those of the World's Ten Largest Economies
Source: World Bank data.

ranks second only to the United States among the population giants.[4] Brazil's PPP annual income was $12,221. This means that Brazil's population has a considerably higher income than does China's ($9,844), Indonesia's ($5,204), or India's ($4,077). This makes Brazil particularly attractive as a market for businesses from outside Brazil (figures 2.4 and 2.5).

Despite these statistics, Brazil has a long way to go before it could be considered a wealthy country. It is relatively wealthy only when compared with its fellow population giants. Brazil's $12,221 PPP annual income is well under a quarter of the United States' $53,101. Brazil has also only one-third of the average of $36,847 for the thirty-four members of the Organization for Economic Cooperation and Development, which more or less represents those countries considered to make up the developed world.

The Challenge of High Density
Although Brazil gains some advantages for business regarding market access, there are many downsides for having such a high population density. Indeed, all these statistics indicate the same overall picture: Brazil faces challenges related to the dense populations of its large cities, where space, mobility, employment, education, and quality of life converge to eat away at its efforts to develop. A few examples will be illustrative.

First, the infrastructure for good roads and highways is so challenging in Brazil that sometimes trucks queuing up to enter the Port of Santos form lines more than 25 miles long.[5] Based on data from the US Central Intelligence Agency's *World Factbook*, Brazil has more than 980,000 miles (1,580,964 kilometers) of highways, of which only 132,226 miles (212,798 kilometers) are paved.[6] That is only 13.4 percent! And this is a country that adds more than 5 million new vehicles to its roads every year. Imagine how frustrating it would be to be able to tap into the latest technologies to grow your crops, and then be limited because you cannot get them to the port for exportation. We know of an American company in Rio de Janeiro that builds deep-sea oil wells. The sizes of the oil wells are not limited by engineering, technology, know-how, or money, but they are limited by the

2.1 São Paulo City
São Paulo, the concrete jungle.

small highways, tunnels, and local roads over which the finished products need to travel when being transported across town.

A second challenge related to population density is the traffic and transportation in Brazil's cities. The country's most developed metro system and rail lines are found in metropolitan São Paulo. But even there, the 194 miles of metro and rail lines are less than half of what exists in such cities as London, Berlin, and New York. And the public rail lines include shared lines for freight transportation. In greater São Paulo alone, there are more than 7 million cars. Wealthy executives are even known to prefer commuting by helicopter, just to avoid the gridlock down below. On November 14, 2013, the traffic monitoring system recorded that São Paulo had a 192-mile traffic jam.[7] There is a total of 539 miles of monitored roads in greater São Paulo, meaning that 35 percent of all road space was used up all over the city.

As a third example of how people move from one place to another, consider how people move around Rio de Janeiro. There are no direct ways to get anywhere in Rio. The city's beaches, mountains, lagoons, bridges, and tunnels converge to make

2.2 São Paulo Traffic
A typical everyday traffic jam in São Paulo.

"direct" an impossible travel option. The Canadian-born coauthor of this book recalls an experience when arriving at Galião–Antonio Carlos Jobim International Airport in Rio, with a plan to stay with friends in nearby Niterói. From Galião, there is a regional shuttle bus that drops passengers off at the ferry that leaves from Praça XV in downtown Rio. From there, the ferry crosses the bay, and finally a taxi was used to arrive at the friend's house. Travel in Rio that day included a plane, bus, boat, and taxi! Additionally in Rio, near the General Osório subway station, a new elevator takes the *favela* residents up to the Morro do Cantagalo. And if you would like to visit the Santa Teresa neighborhood, the *bondinho*, a train-like cable car, is the best way to go. If you are located in Rio's southern zone, near the lagoon, and you want to go to the northern zone, going through the Rebouças Tunnel underneath the mountain is the best way to avoid the old city center. And finally, if you want to go from Rio to Tijuca, going behind the mountains, although longer, is definitely easier than taking the one and only single-lane road that goes up the hill from Leblon to Conrado.

2.3 Rio de Janeiro City
All curves and no straight lines in Rio de Janeiro.

Welcome to a normal day of travel in Rio! It has been said that there are no straight lines in Rio. Everything is a curve. Everything is wavy, from the ocean to the beaches, from the mountain tops to the lagoon, from the sunbathers to the sidewalks. If you are a foreigner doing business in Brazil, be aware that it takes time to get from one location to another. This also affects when meetings start, how long they take, where you take clients to eat, and how long you spend with them.

CRIME AND SAFETY ISSUES

Another way in which the physical environment affects Brazilian culture is how society handles security. Historically, we read of fortresses that had moats around the castle to protect the residents. In Brazil there is something similar in the way that Brazilian homes, apartments, and offices approach security.

Brazilians are often amazed when they see North American residential areas. In the United States we can often walk up and actually touch the walls and doors of American homes.

2.4 A Gated Residence
Secure everything behind walls, gates, and barred enclosures.

Americans park their cars next to the curb right on the street.
Brazil simply has a different look, based on their response to
security concerns. Even in smaller cities and rural areas, homes
that are located in residential locations are surrounded by a wall.
Visitors may *bate palmas* (clap their hands) to get the attention
of the residents, who then give permission to enter the gate.
Homes in larger cities are enclosed by metal gates, metal bars,
barbed wire on roofs and walls, or chunks of broken glass that
are cemented into protection walls. Brazilians park their cars
inside the walled, gated, and barred enclosures. Their steering
wheel is secured, and their stereo systems are removed. Even to
enter into a Brazilian house requires a large number of keys that
wend one through the maze of walls, gates, doors, and openings.
If one lives in an apartment, there is almost always a guard who
welcomes residents home and who serves as the gatekeeper for
visitors and intruders.

On the professional side, do not be surprised by security
measures that become part of your visit to Brazilian companies.
You will be asked to show your passport, have them make copies
of your passport and passport number, write down the time you

enter and exit, have your photo taken, or go through any number of other gatekeeping precautions. If you take money from an automated teller machine, from your North American perspective you will notice that in Brazil all machines are enclosed in a protected area. There are no on-the-street teller machines. When a person uses a credit card at a restaurant, the waitress will bring the machine to your table. Your credit card will never leave your sight. There is simply more attention paid to security issues in Brazil, and they become part of daily activities.

THE CLIMATE AND THE WEATHER

Foreigners who do business in Brazil are often unprepared for the changes in the climate and the weather. First of all, most of Brazil is in the Southern Hemisphere, meaning that its seasons are reversed from those up north. It often takes time to adjust to the fact that when it is summer in New York, it is winter in Porto Alegre. Even in cities like São Paulo and Curitiba, where the temperatures rarely go down to zero, residents begin to feel extremely cold during the winter. Part of the reason is that Brazilian homes and professional buildings often have a flow of outside air. Windows may be open, spaces under doors are wide, gaps in windows are not airtight, and so on. When a person sits in a room where the outside air of 45°F seeps through, things start to feel chilly. Where North Americans tend to modify their comfort by changing a thermostat, Brazilians are more likely to add or remove layers of clothing.

The same is true during the summer months, when Brazilians tend to use air-conditioners less frequently and at higher temperatures than their North American counterparts. Because of brownouts and the costs and availability of electricity, you will find that Brazilians are more sensitive to turning off the air-conditioner (which is usually a wall unit and almost never central cooling), turning off lights, or sitting in rooms that just have natural light. All this means that you may find yourself hotter in the summer and colder in the winter than what one would expect at home.

One of the unique physical features of Brazil is the existence of the capital city of Brasília. Nowhere else in the world is there a capital city that was, by design, built to cause its citizens to look inward and away from its coast and to turn toward the country's vast unpopulated regions. Before 1960 there was no Brasília. Today it is a capital city with a population of more than 2 million. Its design, layout, and architecture are all stunning. It certainly deserves its recognition as a UNESCO World Heritage Site. In a related way, Brasília's modernist architecture, with Oscar Niemeyer as the chief architect, has influenced the look of structures throughout the whole country. In Belo Horizonte, for example, a number of structures were also designed by Niemeyer. Avenida Paulista and Ibirapuera Park in São Paulo also exemplify tremendous modernist influences. Curitiba, in the State of Parana, is Brazil's poster city for a green capital city, mixing parks, forests, and green public spaces with its equally impressive planning for transportation and social sustainability. And let us not fail to mention Recife, the northeastern capital city of Pernambuco State that is exploding with new development in information technology and medical facilities, as well as becoming a manufacturing and exporting hub. It is

2.5 Brasília
Brasília: from zero to 2 million in fifty years.

easy to forget about Recife and focus on the better-known centers
of southeastern Brazil. But if one is looking to see the modern
Brazil, in many ways Recife is leading the pack.

Street art in Brazil is definitely a case where beauty is in the
eye of the beholder. Given that Brazilian cities have so many
walls that surround properties, the walls are often covered with
street art, graffiti, political posters, and advertisements. Some
people love it, and even invite graffiti artists to travel to create
more art; others simply think of it as ugly defacing of public
space. Add to this look the fact that many streets are paved with
cobblestones (*paralelepípedo*) instead of asphalt or concrete. And
add to this picture avocado and mango trees, and you have created the characteristic look and feel of Brazilian cities.

Another feature that non-Brazilians will notice when entering offices and other indoor spaces in Brazil is that the acoustics

seem different. This is partly because there are fewer carpeted floors, more wooden floors, more granite and stone, more sounds from the streets, thinner walls, and more bare concrete. Everything seemingly echoes more. This is also true of Brazilian universities and campuses, which generally are more open to outside temperatures and noises.

Visitors will also sense this same feeling when entering Brazilian airports, museums, and hotels. The truth is that Brazil has yet to develop a solid infrastructure for its tourist industry. Some of the places where this is most evident are its hotels. As compared with North American hotels, the chances are that your Brazilian hotel will feel overpriced because its rooms, bedding, and furniture will be smaller and plainer than expected. This is not to say that there are no fancy and elegant hotels in Brazil, because there are. On balance, however, and especially in second-tier cities, you will find that the price of the hotel does not jibe with your basic sense of expected quality.

ENVIRONMENTAL RESPONSIBILITY

In Brazil it is easy to be green. That is to say, Brazilians have a sensitivity to energy and its effects on daily life. Almost forty years ago, Brazil began experimenting with the production of sugarcane-based fuels. Today Brazil is the world's number one producer of sugarcane. Most of the production comes from the country's South Central region, mainly in the states of São Paulo and Minas Gerais. There is a second pocket in the Northeast, where sugarcane grows as well. About 2 percent of all the arable lands that are available in Brazil are used for growing sugarcane. In addition to sugar and ethanol, Brazil leads the way in producing plastics and electricity that also come from sugarcane. It is not uncommon to see Brazilians who run their cars on gasoline, ethanol, and natural gas. It is entertaining to watch Brazilians drive because they switch back and forth from gasoline to natural gas. That is, if the car needs more power, they will switch to gasoline; but if the car is coasting along a flat stretch of road, they may switch back to natural gas. Do not be surprised when you open up the trunk of a taxi that there will also be a large cylinder tank for the natural gas.

Although many countries still rely on fossil fuels as the main source of their electric power, Brazil enjoys the privilege of having more rivers than most countries. Consequently, Brazil is one of the world's leaders in the production and use of hydropower. Except for years when there are extreme droughts (which do happen in Brazil), in general Brazil depends on hydropower for almost 80 percent of its electricity; by comparison, the United States gets about 7 percent.[8] This may be unexpected, given that Brazil is also one of the world's largest oil producers.

The pre-salt discoveries rank as one of the largest petroleum reserves in the world. The pre-salt region extends along the coast near the states of Rio de Janeiro and Espírito Santo for about 500 miles in length and 125 miles in width. Of course this reserve comes with difficult technical challenges, but it also has the potential to provide Brazil with thousands of jobs and significant amounts of petroleum. If you are a foreigner working with Brazilians, you will find out that though São Paulo is the country's financial center, Rio de Janeiro plays a more central role in energy, especially for petroleum. Conversely, São Paulo is the epicenter of sugarcane production. And when it comes to hydropower, in the early years Brazil focused its attention on gigantic dams (e.g., Itaipu), but nowadays the strategy is to build more, smaller dams in more diverse locations. Those who work with Brazilians in the energy field may find themselves in many different parts of the country.

USING WHAT YOU KNOW ABOUT THE ENVIRONMENT TO ENCOURAGE GOOD COMMUNICATION

As you learn how to assess your environment to improve your communication with Brazilians, use it as an opportunity to focus on the "unseen" yet obvious realities that surround you. Using what we have observed, we suggest the following to help you succeed in your relationships in Brazil.

Enjoy the Ride

We once met an American business executive who had traveled to many parts of the world. She was an experienced traveler who had even lived abroad. However, for whatever reason, when she arrived in São Paulo, she was totally intimidated by the size, density, and rhythm of the city. After hearing many stories of traffic jams, violence, gangs, and poverty, she hunkered down in a hotel, and was incapable of venturing out into the city. No parks, no museums, no restaurants, no music, no sightseeing, and no shopping; she simply hid out in the hotel. How tragic! Instead, our recommendation is to enjoy the ride. São Paulo, for example, despite the logistical difficulties of getting around, boasts hundreds of green areas and parks, fantastic restaurants, incredible shows and nightlife, and fascinating jewels of charming neighborhoods. There is a well-known pop song from the 1960s by one of Brazil's most famous singers, Caetano Veloso. The song, titled "Sampa," tells of Caetano's own version of being shocked by his first impressions of São Paulo, but then slowly beginning to see the beauty behind it all. Take a second peek, beyond the surface, and you will find yourself joining Caetano in singing the praises of São Paulo.

Rio de Janeiro can be equally intimidating, but there the challenge becomes how to blend your activities with the physical environment around you. It makes no sense, for example, to schedule early morning meetings when your Brazilian counterpart takes time to walk her dog along the beach before beginning the workday. Cariocas (as the residents of Rio are called) simply wrap the physical environment of their surroundings into who they are and what they do. So enjoy the ride, and follow suit. At the same time, be aware that unlike the situation in many beach cities in the world, the beaches in Rio are almost all public. Apartments and hotels are separated from the beaches by sidewalks and avenues. The result is that everyone has the right to be on the beach—rich and poor, old and young, fit and flabby, honest and scoundrel. The flip side to the beauty of this openness is that Cariocas have a keen eye for security. They know what to leave at home, when to take taxis instead of walking, and what locations to stay away from. Nonlocals simply do not have the same intuitive sense of these things.

Appreciate Brazil's Physical Diversity

There are twenty-six states in Brazil. Avoid the tendency to put all of Brazil into the same environmental bag. Brazil is simply too large a country, with too diverse a topography, to be able to generalize about its physical environment. Visitors are likely to spend freezing cold nights in Rio Grande do Sul, but also to sweat in what seems like the unearthly hot weather of Teresina, Piauí. The super-humid daytime air in Manaus feels totally different from the crisp night air when looking up at the stars from the mountainous regions of Minas Gerais. You may find yourself squeezing into the subway just as easily as stepping into a rocking ferryboat. In the interior of the State of São Paulo, you may drive for hours and hours, with sugarcane fields as far as the eye can see in every direction. But you may also drive for hours in the city of São Paulo and only see skyscrapers in every direction. Therefore, Brazilians often talk of Brasis, meaning the many different types of Brazil. ("Brasis" means "Brazils"; in Portuguese, words that end in the letter "l" are made plural by dropping the "l" and adding "is.")

Our recommendation is that you give local Brazilians a chance to paint a picture of their region, and of what makes it unique. They will be open to your curiosity and willingness to learn. One brief example: Recently we were traveling in Piauí, in the North of Brazil, with a Brazilian friend who is from Joinville, a city in the southern State of Santa Catarina. While ordering drinks at a restaurant, our Brazilian friend was just as clueless as we were about the names of the various fruit juices. We spent a delightful afternoon learning the names and flavors of many new fruits. Even Brazilians are unfamiliar with all these regional details.

To Stay Safe, Be Aware of Your Surroundings

As to safety precautions, be aware of your surroundings. Brazilian driving is a bit looser with regard to traffic regulations than what one might find in North America. Brazilians often treat red lights as stop signs, and stop signs as yield signs. Motorcycle drivers drive between lanes, and you need to watch out for them. Brazilian drivers, by necessity, are more aggressive. Even as a pedestrian, you need to be more alert to traffic. If you drive in Brazil, parking can be a challenge. Be aware of people on the street who ask for money to watch your car. If you do pay them a couple of dollars, it is best to pay them when you return to the car and not when you initially park.

As to theft, like any large city, Brazilian large cities have quite a bit of petty theft. Brazilians will know what parts of town to avoid and which streets are dangerous. As a foreigner, it is more difficult to know how to tell when you are in the good parts of town and when you are in the bad parts. This is especially difficult to determine in cities like Rio de Janeiro and Salvador. Our recommendation is that you take a taxi, especially at night, if you are in areas that are less familiar. When you go out at night, it is best to travel in groups, take only the money you need for the evening, and leave your flashy watches, rings, and jewelry items at home. Pickpockets are prevalent in the larger cities, especially in high-tourist areas. Do not leave your purse hanging over your shoulder, and do not keep your wallet in your back pocket.

Generally, it is best to keep a copy of your passport with you and to leave the original at home. Women should hold on to their purses, and in fact many restaurants have ways of tying a purse to a chair. Credit card theft is also quite prevalent. It is generally safer to use a bit more cash and use your credit card less frequently. Exercise caution, but do not let your concerns become overly exaggerated.

Be Curious about Why Brazilians Do What They Do

When observing cultural differences, it often helps to assess the reason behind the behavior. That is to say, assume that local people are intelligent. If something seems out of place, it becomes our challenge to discover why people do what they do. For example, in the following photograph of a row of cars parked in front of the São Sebastião Cathedral in Rio de Janeiro, notice that the cars are so close to each other that they actually touch, bumper to bumper. You may wonder how it is possible to park cars in such a way.

Because of the population density and the high number of cars on the road in Rio, parking is extremely difficult. One of

2.7 Parked Cars in Rio de Janeiro
To save space, leave your car in neutral when parking bumper to bumper.

the solutions is to leave your parked car in neutral. There is a person who watches over the cars, and who literally pushes a few forward or a few backward when a driver returns to his or her vehicle. For a small fee, drivers know that their car will be taken care of, and it also helps to know that someone is watching to make sure that nobody breaks into a parked car. In this way Cariocas are able to park more cars in a limited space. This creative response to a problem is a perfect example of a cultural difference that is based on the environment, and one that at first seems illogical. As such, our third recommendation is that you learn to observe what is around you and search for the motive behind it.

WRAPPING IT UP

The environment category of LESCANT can be challenging because it encompasses such a diverse array of items. Still, the benefit comes in helping people observe what is around us, and in adjusting our intercultural communication because of these observations.

What we know about Brazil's environment:

Topography and size
- Fifth-largest country in the world.
- Larger than the continental United States.
- 20 percent of the world's oxygen comes from the Amazon rain forest.
- The Amazon River is the world's largest, in terms of flow.

Population and density
- More than 200 million people.
- Dense urban population, sparse rural population.
- Poorly developed roads and highways.

Crime and safety issues
- Gated and fenced residences and businesses are common.
- Doormen and security personnel are also common.
- Automated teller machines are always enclosed.
- Petty theft is common.
- Fear of car thefts means that many security precautions are taken.
- Credit cards are used cautiously.

Climate and weather
- The seasons are reversed (compared with the Northern Hemisphere).
- There are both tropical and subtropical areas.
- There are both deserts and wetlands.
- There is often no central air-conditioning or heating.
- People wear layers of clothing instead of changing the thermostat.

Architecture, buildings, and office space
- The country has a planned, creative capital city—Brasília.
- Oscar Niemeyer was Brasília's architect.
- Brasília has cobblestone streets, and building and graffiti art.

Environmental responsibility
- A sensitivity to being green.
- There has been a forty-year history of sugarcane-based fuels.
- Given the number of rivers, there is a high dependence on hydropower.
- 80 percent of Brazil's electricity comes from hydropower (compared with 7 percent in the United States)
- Brazil's pre-salt petroleum reserves are among the world's largest.

Communication strategies on how to succeed in Brazil's environment:

- Enjoy the ride. Do not let the population density, talk of crime, and lack of infrastructure keep you from getting out among the people.

- Appreciate the twenty-six states and multiple regions with diverse ways of life.
- Be safe—especially, be vigilant in traffic and about possible petty thieves; at night, travel in groups and take taxis.
- Assume that Brazilians have good reasons for doing what they do.

3

BRAZILIAN
Social
Organization

Let's Work On It Together

When we look at social organization, we look at how society is put together. We build on this feature by focusing on how institutions and collective activities are shared by members of a culture. There are many ways in which a society subdivides itself to create a sense of community: family, education, the role of women, religion, how people spend their leisure time, and so on. These are all culturally based. As we review some of these areas within a Brazilian context, we gain a better appreciation of how significant these social groups are.

Let us begin by looking at Brazilian perceptions of kinship and family. We then look at education, the class system, gender roles, issues of race, individualism versus collectivism, religion, and finally sports. Along the way, we offer general recommendations. And we end the chapter with specific recommendations related to social organization.

One of the major ways that societies subdivide themselves is by families. Brazil is a country that has historically had strong family ties, where there is loyalty to siblings, attention to parents as they get older, and a sense of obligation that goes with caring for grandparents and others of the *terceira idade* (the third generation). In the United States, when people think of the nuclear family, generally we think of two generations: parents and children. In Brazil, however, the nuclear family at the very least also includes the grandparents. As a result, by comparison, in the United States if one asks grandparents to live in the home with the family, there is a sense that we are going out of our way to be extremely helpful. It is not that people do not take care of their family, but to have grandparents live in the home is seen as quite a sacrifice. In Brazil there is a greater expectation that the grandparents will be living in the home with their children and grandchildren. It is less of a sacrifice and more of the expected norm.

The following photograph was taken in Salvador, Bahia, in a neighborhood that has a Faculdade da Felicidade (Happiness College), which offers training, courses, lectures, and a host of other activities for the elderly. The name of the institution is a clever play on words. In Portuguese *idade* means "age," but *-idade* also happens to be the suffix at the end of the adjective, *feliz* (happy), that turns the word into a noun, *felicidade* (happiness).

Faculdade da Felicidade
Onde ser feliz é uma conquista da maturidade

www.faculdadedafelicidade.com.br
de telefones: (71) 3015-4522 / (71) 8132-9539   @Fac_felic

3.1 The Happy Age
Felicidade—a play on words, meaning "happiness" or the "happy age."

In other words, the institute's name could also be interpreted as the College of the Happy Age. As related to social organization, this is a good example of how the elderly are watched over by their families.

There are other examples that illustrate the focus that Brazil gives to the elderly and to families. The following photos were taken in the parking lot of a Pão de Açúcar supermarket in São Paulo. In front of the market, there are special parking spots for the elderly and for pregnant women. In North America we frequently see parking spots that are reserved for the handicapped, but not for the elderly and pregnant. These photographs say a

3.2 Parking for the Elderly
Special parking spots at supermarkets for the elderly.

3.3 Parking for Those Who Are Expecting
Special parking spots at supermarkets for pregnant women.

3.4 Exercise Machines for the Elderly
Public parks with exercise equipment for the elderly.

lot about the values that Brazilians put on these people. Special deference is given to elderly and pregnant women.

There are also many parks in Brazil that offer public activities for the elderly. In photo 3.4, we see a park that contains exercise equipment especially designed for the elderly, including instructions on how to use it. The park is located right in the center of the old downtown region in Rio de Janeiro. This is quite common in Brazil, and other cities also have special areas in parks that are set aside with exercise equipment designed for use by the elderly.

The next example (photo 3.5) is a photo that was taken in a Carrefour supermarket. There is a special checkout line that reads *Gestantes, mulheres c/crianças de colo, idosos, e deficientes têm preferência de atendimento* (Pregnant women, women with small children, elderly, and handicapped have preference in being served). This sign reveals Brazilian values. Unlike North American supermarkets, which have checkout lines that are based on the number of items to be purchased (showing a value on efficiency of time use), the Brazilian sign shows a value that is given to specific members of their society.

As related to family, it is also true that North American families are more apt to have their young adult children move away.

3.5 Special Needs at the Supermarket
Supermarket lines for those with special needs.

They may go away to school. They may move to another city for a job. They may even move to another apartment in the same city, simply because it is a sign of their independence. In Brazil it is still more common for children to continue living at home, until marriage, even if this marriage does not happen until a child is more than thirty years of age.

FAMILY AND PROFESSIONAL SERVICES

Brazilians depend heavily on relatives for connections for professional services. If someone needs a lawyer, an architect, an accountant, or a supplier for a family business, Brazilians will look first at a relative. Brazil has thousands of family-owned businesses, and most Brazilians will hire family members to cover a multitude of professional tasks. Brazilians do not share the negative connotation that North Americans associate with nepotism. Brazilians, by contrast, have a positive feeling about relying on family ties because in Brazil such family ties increase obligation and a desire to help. To a Brazilian's way of thinking, a relative who has the family name to protect is going to work harder than a complete stranger who has no family connection.

There is another issue at play here as well. Although there has been radical improvement in this regard in the last twenty years or so, Brazil has traditionally struggled with corruption in law enforcement, government, and the courts. Because many Brazilians came to feel that they could not trust legal action to ensure compliance with contracts or business agreements, they turned to family loyalties to ensure fair and honest dealings among each other.

All this stands in direct contrast to US and Canadian views of nepotism as something bad. North Americans see nepotism as inherently unfair and susceptible to favoritism. In North America people tend to see nepotism as a way to protect incompetent relatives or to take advantage of non–family members. This, in turn, reduces productivity and diminishes accountability. In Brazil the opposite is true. Family loyalties actually tend to increase productivity and ensure accountability. Multinational companies—especially when creating connections, mergers, and acquisitions of Brazilian companies—would do well to keep the sense of family obligations in mind.

EDUCATION

One of Brazil's greatest challenges is related to the education of its young people. North Americans seldom appreciate the incredible infrastructure for education that is available in the United States. In the United States a young student could be the worst student in high school, at the bottom of the academic pile; yet still, with a diploma in hand, this person will have options for higher education. It may not be at the most prestigious school, but there will be local colleges and universities that this person can attend. There are literally thousands of schools.

The situation in Brazil is much different. The growing population of young people, combined with the limited number of institutions of higher education, has created a bottleneck of sorts in the country's ability to continue education. Currently, when students complete high school, rather than directly enter a university, they prepare for a college entrance exam called the *vestibular*. The preparation course is called the *cursinho*, and students take a full year for it. Additionally, unlike the North American ACT or SAT, which is a general exam for everyone, Brazilian students prepare for a specific *vestibular* at a specific school for a specific subject. That is to say, for example, if a student wants to study law at the University of São Paulo, she must prepare for that university's law *vestibular*. If she is lucky enough to be accepted, but then decides that the law is not what she wants to study, this student cannot simply change programs. Instead, she would need to take the *vestibular* in the other area. Even if this student loves law, but then needs to move to another city, she would need to take the *vestibular* for the law program at the new university. (Law is an undergraduate degree in Brazil.)

The result of all this is that it becomes much more difficult to get into higher education in Brazil. There simply are not enough openings for the number of students who would like to study. There is no undergraduate concept of general education, and clearly there is no possibility to have an undeclared major or to change your major two or three times along the way. Brazil has recently addressed this challenge by creating a program called Ciência sem fronteiras (Science without Borders). The objective is to increase the number of students who study abroad, who will then bring their skills back to Brazil in order to provide the infrastructure for professional work and for future higher education. More than a hundred thousand students are expected to study in the United States alone, and others are encouraged to study in many other countries around the world. In recent years some universities in Brazil have also shifted toward a standardized national examination called the Exame Nacional do Ensino Médio. This test is not without controversy, but its general concept hopes to help streamline national standards and democratize access to institutions of higher education.

THE CLASS SYSTEM

One of the most significant changes in Brazil in recent years is the rising middle class, including their increased spending and consumption. After decades of political uncertainty, external debt, and hyperinflation, new stability has created an environment where millions have been added to the middle class. In 1994 Brazil's annual gross domestic product income at purchasing power parity was $3,425 per person. By 2004 this figure had hardly budged, reaching $3,607. But just three years later, in 2007, the figure had nearly doubled, to just under $7,200. By 2011 the 1994 figure had tripled, to more than $12,500. Currently (in 2016, as this book goes to press), the figure has slipped slightly, but remains a healthy $11,208.[1]

Those interested in investing in Brazil are attracted by the allure of its new middle class. However, it is good to use caution when interpreting what it means to be middle class in Brazil. In Brazil those who move out of poverty (called Classe D) and enter the middle class (called Classe C) cross the threshold of making more than about $750 a month, which would give them about $9,000 a year. Because, for several years now, the average per capita income in Brazil has been higher than this (as discussed above), the average Brazilian is now officially in the middle class. Nevertheless, though Brazil has made remarkable progress, it would be a mistake for us to think of "middle class" with the same mindset as for other developed countries. We might make the mistake of assuming that Brazilians are now earning something like $42,590 a year, as in Canada, or $53,960, as in the United States, which just is not so. Brazil, for that matter, ranks only third in South America in per capita annual income, behind Uruguay ($18,930) and Chile ($21,030). That said, it is hard to compare incomes directly in this way. This is because the cost of living in Brazil is much lower than in these more mature economies. For instance, at the time of this writing (2016), average consumer prices were more than 20 percent higher in the United States than in Brazil, groceries were just under 60 percent higher in the United States than in Brazil, and rent was more than 68 percent as expensive in Brazil as in the United States.[2] In other words, that same $11,000 annual income in Brazil stretches considerably farther than it would in the United States.

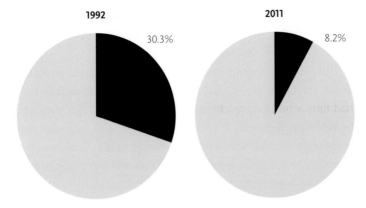

1992

2011

30.3%

8.2%

Figure 3.1
Brazilians Living in Extreme Poverty, 1992 and 2011
Source: World Bank data.

Related to this is the remarkable progress Brazil has made in reducing the number of people living in extreme poverty (here defined as living on $2.00 a day). In 1992 almost a third—30.3 percent—of Brazil's people lived on just $2.00 or less a day. In just a decade, by 2002, that proportion had fallen to just 20.2 percent. In 2011 (the most recent year for which there are reliable data), it had fallen much further, to 8.2 percent (figure 3.1). Although almost a tenth of the population living in extreme poverty is still unacceptably high, this nonetheless shows enormous progress. Moreover, this progress means greater buying power and a growing consumer market within Brazil.

To put this fully in perspective, Brazil fares much better now than the other emerging market powerhouses such as China, where 27.2 percent of the people lived on $2.00 a day (in 2010) and far better than India, where the proportion of people living on $2.00 in 2010 was 68.9 percent. Still, no one in either Canada or the United States lives on less than $2.00 a day.[3]

Another issue to consider here is the income inequality in Brazil, which has been a major factor in the rise of the Brazilian consumer class. This is a particularly important issue because for much of the 1980s Brazil had among the highest income inequality of any nation in the world. In 1989 the richest

20 percent of Brazil's population held 67.5 percent of the country's wealth. By 2013 that proportion had dropped to 51.9 according to the 2012 GINI Index.[4]

It is true that more Brazilians are opening bank accounts, using credit cards, buying more goods, making online purchases, and shifting to higher-level goods, but all this needs to be interpreted from a Brazilian perspective and not from that of the averages that are common in, for example, Canada or the United States. This is actually a common mistake made among those who hope to do business with Brazilians.

GENDER ROLES

A few years ago, during a consulting visit in Rio de Janeiro, we were invited to have lunch with a group of Brazilian executives. Before this visit, none of us had met the Brazilian team, which consisted of three Brazilian women and two Brazilian men. During the lunch, one of the Brazilian executives began to discuss her latest plastic surgery. She discussed her various annual tucks and lifts with the casualness with which we ask for water to be served. It was an interesting conversation because, as North Americans, we usually exert care to not say things that might be perceived as sexist. The Brazilians, however, openly discussed the need for women to be beautiful, as part of their way of being professional. In light of this conversation, it might not come as a surprise that a 2010 study showed that Brazil ranked fourth in the world in the amount of plastic surgery performed as a percentage of the population.[5]

In some ways, by North American standards, this conversation was as uncomfortable as it was fascinating. We share this experience not to say that women in Brazil do not struggle with issues of blurring sexism and professionalism, but to point out a different worldview. Brazilians are more open about combining issues such as being feminine and being professional. For that matter, Brazilian men give considerably more attention to issues of appearing masculine while being professional than their North American counterparts are likely to do. In North

American culture, there is an effort (realized or not) to ignore differences in gender when dealing with professional matters. In Brazilian culture, there is an effort to recognize feminine and masculine, mixed in with professional matters.

You will find that Brazilians refer to a person's looks and dress frequently. Women notice how manicured another woman's fingernails are. Employees at offices have "uniforms" that seem more revealing and more tight-fitting than what one would expect. People discuss body types and shapes a lot. Job descriptions include information about what physical characteristics the employee should have. Women are expected to act feminine, and men are expected to give them consideration. Of course, all these things are "noticed" in other cultures as well. The difference you will find is in how much Brazilians talk openly about these differences.

When entering the office of a company in Brazil, expect to be met by somebody in a uniform, and this is common to all who work reception areas. Usually the businesses will have guidelines for makeup, hair, and other accessories. There is an attitude that those who first receive clients and customers represent the face of the company. In North American culture, we see something similar in the dress of flight attendants, but less for other companies like insurance, banks, accounting firms, and computer-related jobs.

Neither the Brazilian approach nor the North American approach to these issues reflects any sort of lesser or greater sexism in the society. North Americans, for instance, accept many such gender-based differences as being free of sexist undertones. For example, it is much more acceptable for women to wear nylons and a skirt than for men to do so; yet this differentiation does not demonstrate a sexist tendency. In other words, the fact that Brazilians tend to pay more attention than North Americans to the gender differences in appearance and behavior that are normal in their society should not be seen as somehow right or wrong. Yet this is exactly what happens when gender-based behavior is legally codified, as it is with US or Canadian laws that deal with sexual harassment in terms of a hostile work environment. Brazil, Canada, and the United States equally hold as unlawful quid pro quo sexual harassment (i.e., trading job benefits for sex or harm at work for refusing sex). By contrast, both Canada and the United States have laws that protect against a sexual hostile work environment, covering behavior that is culturally specific to their countries, and that is conversely not felt to be harassment—or even offensive—in Brazil (along with most of the rest of Latin America).

UNDERSTANDING COMPLIMENTS

Brazilians regularly compliment one another on their appearance in a way that is both polite and appreciated. The same compliment in the United States or Canada, by contrast, is not only considered impolite but may result in a lawsuit for sexual harassment. It is, for example, quite common for Brazilian men to regularly compliment the women with whom they work on their hair styling, outfit, or jewelry. In such cases, the men have no intention of true flirtation. Such compliments are simply polite behavior, and the Brazilian women—far from being offended—are usually pleased. By contrast, in the US or Canadian workplace, such comments are indeed offensive. In such cases, the American or Canadian woman is likely to feel that the compliment is sexual in nature. Unlike her Brazilian counterpart, she is likely to feel that the man complimenting her is focusing on her appearance rather than on her work performance. This is because in both North American countries, people make a distinction between work performance and personal appearance or gender-based differences. In Brazil, no such distinction exists.

Nor is this simply true only in one direction. Brazilian women also compliment male workers on their appearance in the workplace. Here, too, the man involved is unlikely to consider this an actual sexual advance. In the United States and Canada, such comments are equally unlawful, and would be interpreted quite differently as open flirtation when it is not. All this is to say that major cultural differences exist between Brazil and North America regarding what is appropriate business communication when gender differences are involved.

Some cultures try to minimize gender differences, while others emphasize them. In general, Brazil emphasizes these kinds of differences more than, for example, the United States. Our recommendation is that you not impose a North American judgment on your perceptions about Brazilian attitudes toward gender roles in professional settings. That is to say, Brazilians are not more sexist simply because of the way they may discuss things more openly.

RACE

From the perspective of a non-Brazilian, one of the most difficult issues to understand about Brazil is how Brazilians talk about and identify race. On one hand, Brazil paints a picture of racial equality, where race is never a social issue. Brazil calls itself a "postracial" society and prides itself on racial equality. On the other hand, Brazil can feel like a country that has deep, hidden, and camouflaged racism that bubbles below the surface. The first thing a foreigner will notice is the open way that people refer to race and physical characteristics in talking about others.

Coming from a North American perspective, it takes a while to get used to the references to people's color. For example, a member of the woman's national soccer team was named Pretinha (little black one). It just seems out of place to have her name written on the back of her jersey. There is a famous duet of singers from the interior of São Paulo State named João Mulato e Douradinho (João Mulatto and Little Toasty). There is a level of shock that goes with hearing the names of these singers. Recently, we took a group of American MBA students on a business tour of Brazil. As part of their experience, they were taking samba lessons. The instructor told them that the dance was not just a matter of learning the steps but also a matter of having an attitude. They needed to have a *negão* (big black one) attitude. (We should add that in Portuguese, the word *negro*—black—simply means the color black and carries none of the social weight that it does in English. Still, it takes some getting used to when people are commonly referred to as *negão*.) All this is to say that Brazil is a country where terms related to a person's physical appearance are openly expressed in ways that in other cultures might be more held back.

The identity of race is especially difficult in Brazil. When Brazilians are born, their birth certificate will have a space for their race, which generally will fall into the categories of *negro* (black), *pardo* (tan), *branco* (white), *asiático* (Asian), or *indígena* (indigenous). The fact that Brazil as a government officially keeps track of race in this way is one argument against the country being the postracial society that many Brazilians claim it to be. What is also interesting here is that the race with which people self-identify may not reflect their actual race. Several studies have shown that a much higher percentage of Brazilians have Sub-Saharan African genetic markers than the percentages self-identified as such in the population.[6]

What is telling here is not only that people self-identify differently than their actual genetic race may indicate but also that Brazilian scientists care enough about this subject to have researched it in the first place. Brazilians are thus more likely to feel more sensitivity regarding the subject of race than the initial visitor to Brazil might suspect from casual conversation.

That said, self-identification is probably the aspect that matters here, and it is worthwhile for this reason to indicate just what the racial breakdown in Brazil is. In the last government survey on race, 48.9 percent of Brazilians self-identified as white, 43.1 percent as *pardo*, 6.3 percent as black, 0.5 percent as Asian, and 0.4 percent as Amerindian or indigenous (figure 3.2).

Aside from just the racial composition of Brazil, and the evidence for some sensitivity in how people self-categorize, there is the way Brazilians use race to describe themselves in general conversations. For instance, some Brazilians use many other terms to describe a person's race—*moreno, mulato, café com leite, cabo verde*, and so on. When asked about a person's race, many Brazilians start by saying, "My birth certificate says that I am *pardo*, but I consider myself *negro*." For some Brazilians, terms like *negro, pardo, moreno, mulato, café com leite*, and *cabo verde* are simply camouflaged evidence of racism, and their general opinion is that everyone should just be called *negro*. For others, these terms carry no more weight than blonde, brunette, and redhead do in English.

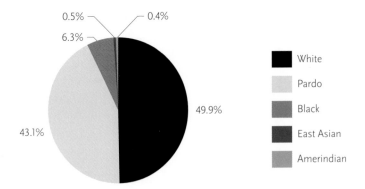

Figure 3.2
Self-Reported Race in Brazil, 2006
Source: Instituto Brasileiro de Geografia e Estatística.

There is a famous story that once the soccer player Neymar was asked if he had ever been a victim of racial prejudice. His answer was something like "No, never, neither on the field nor off the field. But then, it's because I'm not really black, right?" There was quite a stir afterward because people assumed that he was black, or that he would at least identify himself as being black. Given examples like this, it is easy to see why it is confusing to understand race identity in Brazil.

Similarly, notice that in Brazil there is no category for Hispanic or Latino. Brazilians simply do not relate to the issues of when a term like "Hispanic" and when a term like "Latino" would be applicable. In fact, someone who is identified as Hispanic in the United States would be identified in the Brazilian census as white.

Photo 3.6 was taken on Copacabana Beach in Rio de Janeiro. There is a sign that recommends to beachgoers what level of sunblock protection should be worn, based on the intensity of the sun. The recommended protection levels are divided into four categories: *mulatos e negros* (mulattoes and blacks), *morenos escuros* (dark dark-skinned), *morenos claros* (light dark-skinned), and *ruivos e loiros* (redheads and blonds). The fact that people need different levels of sun protection is not the issue. What is interesting is to see how Brazilians use the terms, mixing skin color and race.

3.6 Sunblock Protection for Beachgoers
Recommended sunblock protection for beachgoers with different skin tones.

In recent years Brazil has begun affirmative action programs, especially targeting students who would like to continue their education at universities. As part of this process, there have been adjustments to how people identify themselves (especially in terms of *pardo* vs. *negro*). Students are now allowed to self-determine if they are *negro*. In reality, this means that some who would previously have referred to themselves as *pardo* now identify themselves as *negro*. Other Brazilians now identify themselves as *negro*, simply because they have become more sensitive to the prejudicial undertones of words like *mulato* or *pardo*. A large part of this is related to the level of discomfort that is associated with the various terms that subdivide Brazilians into various levels of blackness.

One final observation about race: We have focused on issues of blackness, but Brazil is a nation of immigrants from all over the world. Many of them form networks in business and social circles, and all of them contribute to the tapestry that makes up Brazil's rich cultural diversity.

WHERE ARE BRAZILIANS FROM?

Although the largest percentage of Brazilians claim descent from Portugal, there are seven other ethnic groups in Brazil with more than 1 million people: those who self-identify as Italians (13.1 percent of the population), Spaniards (7.8 percent),

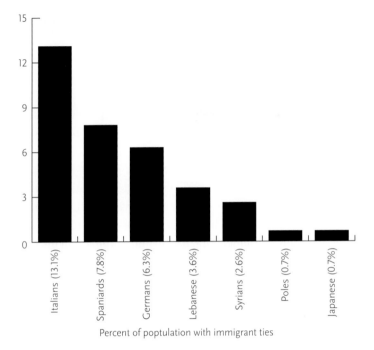

Figure 3.3

Brazilians Have Strong Immigrant Ethnic Ties, with Seven Ethnic Groups of More
Than 1 Million

Source: Instituto Brasileiro de Geografia e Estatística.

Germans (6.3 percent), Lebanese (3.6 percent), Syrians (2.6 percent), Poles (0.7 percent), and Japanese (0.7 percent). For all these groups, many Brazilians maintain cultural ties even after they have lost their linguistic ones (figure 3.3).

On a national scale, some of the groups may seem fairly small, but they can be significant regionally. For instance, though only 0.5 percent of Brazilians self-identify as Asian, there are more than 1 million people of Japanese descent in Brazil. In fact, São Paulo alone has more than 325,000 people of Japanese descent, the largest population outside Japan itself. These numbers, by the way, are flexible depending on the context in which people self-identify. For instance, in government records of self-identification, all East Asians (i.e., not just Japanese but also Chinese, Korean, and others) come to 0.5 percent,

BRAZILLIAN SOCIAL ORGANIZATION

whereas in ethnic identification, Brazilians of Japanese descent self-identify as 0.7 percent.

There are also large portions of Brazilians with ethnic group identities from the Arabic-speaking world, especially from Syria and Lebanon (which, combined, constitute 6.2 percent of the population). In fact, with more than 1 million people claiming Arabic heritage, Brazil has the highest number of Arab citizens outside the Middle East.

Brazil's largest non-Portuguese ethnic group comes from Italy, with 13.1 percent of Brazilians self-identifying as Italian. Because the government of Italy recognizes the children of Italians born in Brazil to be Italian citizens, many of these are dual nationals. Although Brazil's 30-million-plus Italians live throughout the country, some areas are more heavily Italian ethnically than others. More Italians live in São Paulo State than anywhere else in Brazil, with just under 10 million people claiming Italian descent, representing 30 percent of its population. Other states have smaller populations but higher percentages. For instance, the 2.7 million Italian Brazilians living in Santa Catarina make up 60 percent of the state's population, whereas the 1.7 million living in Minas Gerais make up a whopping 65 percent.[7]

Significant groups of people also have heritage and roots in Poland and Germany. And of course, thousands have ancestors all over other parts of the world as well. Finally, large areas of Brazil's sparsely populated interior have high percentages of their population with Amerindian heritage. These indigenous people in Brazil present an extremely complex mix of hundreds of tribes.

You need to be aware that Brazilians are extremely open about race, but are also extremely closed about discussing racial issues. By comparison, North Americans aggressively talk about race. From civil war to civil rights, from famous court trials to famous athletes, racial issues have been portrayed in the US media for years. Brazilians simply have not had an open forum in the way that North Americans have. Our own assessment is that this is changing in Brazil, but you will still find Brazilians less engaged in the discussion.

At the McCombs School of Business, there is a room where a number of promotional posters are displayed. The posters are designed to show the advantages of studying business at the University of Texas. One of the posters shows the famous "hook 'em Horns" sign with the caption "Individual Opportunity." The poster is an excellent example of how North American, and Texan, cultures value individuality. The poster is saying, in essence, that if a student comes to the University of Texas, he or she will be able to do what is best for him or her. That is, the focus is on the individual. There is a belief, in this context, that when individuals are allowed to take advantage of their personal opportunities, society in general will be better off as well.

Brazil, however, is more collectivist in how it sees the role of people in society. As an example of this, along Avenida Paulista in São Paulo there is a building that has a number of bronze plaques. One of these plaques, shown in the photo below, depicts a view from above where we see eight people sitting around a table. The caption that accompanies the plaque says *Só no grupo*

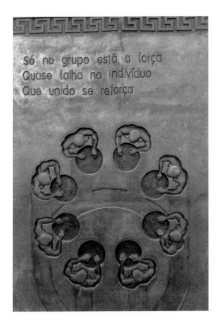

3.7 Strength in the Group
Only in the group is there strength.

está a força. Quase falha no indivíduo que unido se reforça (Only in the group is there strength. Where the individual almost fails, united he is strengthened).

The plaque actually effectively depicts the Brazilian sentiment that all are better off when we unite as a group. Individual desires are important, but are subordinate to the needs of the group. This is not to say that Brazilian thinking is as collectivist as what we see among many in the Asian cultures; but compared with the norms of North America, Brazil does have more collectivist characteristics.

WHAT IS SO GREAT ABOUT COLLECTIVISM?

One question that someone coming from an individualist perspective may have is, How can a group benefit from collectivist thinking? This next photo, 3.8, was taken at the factory of Natura Cosméticos in São Paulo. Natura is the leading manufacturer of beauty products in Brazil. It has a direct sales model, with over a million *consultoras* (consultants) who have a sense of family

3.8 Natura's Consultant Board
Natura consultants who have visited the home office.

within the company. From the company website, these consultants have access to their own blogs, chats, and magazines. In fact, whenever a consultant visits the home office and factory in São Paulo, there is an opportunity to put your name on a round plaque, which is added to the wall of thousands of other consultants who have visited the home office.

Natura not only has a strong sense of belonging to a group, but the company has a unique sense of the quality of life that is shared by the employees. Like many modern factories, Natura's home office has child care facilities, medical doctors on site, a building that promotes ecologically responsible construction, drugstores, lunchroom facilities, and a host of other services. The following photo, however, is unique in what is not seen. This photo was taken during lunchtime. Note that instead of having shifts, whose workers take lunch breaks at different times, at Natura the factory line actually closes down completely during lunchtime. There is a philosophy that everyone's quality of life will increase when everyone takes time off for lunch together. They could increase production by keeping the factory in operation with different shifts, but instead there has been a

3.9 Closing Down for Lunch
The Natura factory line closes down for lunch.
Note: The glare in the photo comes from taking the photo from behind a window.

conscious decision to close things down. This is an excellent example of collectivist thinking, and one that fits well within a Brazilian mindset.

The Takeaway

For those who work with Brazilians, especially for those who come from the United States, it is important to remember that Brazilians do have a greater sense of doing what is good for the whole group. Individual sacrifices are made for the good of others. Individualism, self-reliance, independence, and freedom all have positive connotations for those who come from individualist cultures. However, these same words carry an almost arrogant and conceited connotation for those people who have more of a collectivist orientation. Be aware that "looking out for number one" may not be as popular in Brazil.

RELIGION

Brazil is the world's largest Roman Catholic country. With a population of 200 million, estimates are that 123 million of them are Roman Catholic. When the pope visits Brazil, they fill the beaches of Copacabana with millions of people, just as if it were a Rod Stewart or Rolling Stones concert. The actual number of Roman Catholics is dropping, and many Protestant churches, especially evangelical ones, are gaining in numbers.[8] However, the Roman Catholic religion plays a large role in Brazilian life, especially in its holidays and festivals. Even Carnaval has religious beginnings.

Foreigners who work with Brazilians will observe quite a blending of religion and daily life. Soccer players cross themselves and pray in public. Actors who are interviewed by the media make references to how much God has helped them. Government buildings and offices have many crosses hanging on the walls. City buses have a copy of the Ten Commandments written on the window behind the bus driver. Coworkers invite their friends to witness baptisms and other religious events. This is not to say that Brazilian Catholics attend church services to a high degree, and their focus may not be on doctrine; but it is

3.10 Igreja de Nosso Senhor de Bom Fim
The Igreja de Nosso Senhor de Bom Fim in Salvador.

to say that there is more of a mixing of religious references into their daily activities. Even the Portuguese language is peppered with hundreds of expressions that have Catholic origins—Nossa Senhora, Ai meu Deus, Cruzes, Credo, and so on.

Photo 3.10 was taken at the Igreja de Nosso Senhor de Bom Fim in Salvador. This most famous church in all Bahia presents one of the great examples of Brazilian syncretism when, yearly, the steps of the church are ritually cleaned by the faithful, who combine Roman Catholicism with the Candomblé religion (which originated in Salvador, Bahia, among enslaved Africans who came from Yoruba-speaking regions of Africa) at the Lavagem do Bom Fim. From a North American perspective, it may sound strange to hear a person say that she is both Roman Catholic and Candomblé; but as a social phenomenon, there is less of a conflict with this in Brazil. Also, at this cathedral there is a tremendous display of wax and plastic body parts that represent parts of the body that were miraculously healed, as an answer to their prayers. These are found together with handwritten notes and other *votos* to express gratitude.

The Takeaway

We suggest that foreigners enjoy all the religious celebrations that Brazil has to offer. One need not be Catholic to have a great time at the Festas de São João or at Carnaval. The beauty behind Candomblé is easier to appreciate when one has a little understanding of the characteristics of the various *orixás*. And it is motivating to witness the sincerity and passion of the *evangélicos*. At the same time, if you expect Brazilians to explain their religious beliefs, there will be less of a doctrinal approach and more of a social connection.

SPORTS

Sports and athletics provide a sense of camaraderie, and they are another important part of Brazilian identity. Many Brazilians are fitness minded. Thousands jog, ride bikes, walk along the beach, work out at the gym, and do a lot to keep their bodies in shape. Try going to Ibirapuera Park in São Paulo on the weekend, and you will be joined by thousands of people who are exercising. Go to the beaches in Rio de Janeiro and be joined by all the fitness-conscious people. Brazilians love Formula One, basketball, volleyball, and swimming—but of course the champion of them all is *futebol* (soccer).

One of the first questions that one Brazilian will ask another one is what soccer team he or she supports. Flamengo, from Rio de Janeiro, is the most popular team in all Brazil. Corinthians, from São Paulo, is a close second. There is an instant bond between people based on soccer. Every city has one or two teams, and locally people choose sides. When in São Paulo, you will discuss Corinthians versus Palmeiras, Santos, and São Paulo. When in Rio de Janeiro, you will debate Flamengo versus Vasco, Fluminense, and Botafogo. Once a Brazilian has a team, there is little chance of him or her ever changing. And just try marrying into a family that cheers for another team and see what that starts! We can almost guarantee that soccer will be one of the major ways that you will connect with Brazilian colleagues. Photo 3.11 shows a little girl who has started life with Fluminense, and chances are that she will never change.

3.11 Born to Be Victorious
This little girl *nasceu para vencer*, that is, was "born to be victorious."

Soccer inspires a different level of emotion than most North American sports. Of course, in the United States there are super fans who have a never-ending passion for their favorite teams. However, Brazilian soccer comes with a higher dose of emotion and a lower dose of analysis. The announcers have more passion in their voices. The replays are all in slow motion, including the slow-motion reactions of the fans. A final score of 0 to 0 can still come from a game that was exciting, and a score of 5 to 0 probably means that the game was not very good. North American sports have more of an analytical side. Baseball fans, for example, can give you thousands of statistics—batting percentages, base-stealing percentages, runs batted in with runners on base when there are two out, and so on. Some bring scorecards to the stadium and keep stats during the game. Even the way that announcers give the play-by-play has an analytical style.

The Takeaway

As a foreigner, you do not need to love soccer, but you will earn great connections with Brazilians if you at least try to understand the game. Our recommendation is that you choose a team, learn about some of the players, find out when the season is, and become part of the hoopla. There are plenty of Brazilians who could care less about soccer, but there are plenty of others who do.

RECOMMENDATIONS: USING WHAT YOU KNOW ABOUT SOCIAL ORGANIZATION TO ENCOURAGE GOOD COMMUNICATION

In this chapter we have looked at some of the ways in which Brazilians divide themselves in society. Our approach opens up a way to categorize these cultural differences based on these different groupings. However, none of this is helpful without observation. Our key challenge as foreigners who visit Brazil is to make sure that we observe what is around us and find out what seems to be culturally different. If we do that, then our task becomes figuring out why people do what they do. As you make these observations, we offer three recommendations.

First: Be Flexible in Accepting Differences

Begin from the premise that people are intelligent, and if something seems to be put together "wrong," there must be a good reason. The undertaking then becomes to figure out what that reason is. For example, the following photo was taken in Teresina, Piauí, in the North of Brazil. In Teresina it is common to get around town in motorcycle taxis, as shown in photo 3.12.

In purely North American terms, one might think that this is a dangerous or inefficient way to travel. However, when one considers the size of the city, the number of cars on the road, the quality of the roads, the price of gas, and any other number of factors, one begins to see the logic behind the *mototáxi*. Our first recommendation is that we be flexible in accepting that there are good reasons behind cultural behaviors, and we then try to figure out that reason.

Second: Identify the Values That Are behind Certain Behaviors

How a society organizes itself tells us a lot about what its members value. In this chapter we saw examples of this as related to

3.12 Motorcycle Taxis
There is a certain local logic to traveling by motorcycle taxi.

3.13 Obese Seating on Buses
Yes, the obese are given preferential seating.

ASSENTO PREFERENCIAL PARA OBESOS, GESTANTES,
PESSOAS COM BEBÊS OU CRIANÇAS DE COLO,
IDOSOS E PESSOAS COM DEFICIÊNCIA
AUSENTES PESSOAS NESSAS CONDIÇÔES, O USO É LIVRE.

kinship and family, and in the examples on gender roles. Photo 3.13 was taken in the front seat of a tour bus. The front seat is reserved for those with special needs. Based on the icons, we are not surprised to see that the seat is reserved for the handicapped, the elderly, mothers with small children, and pregnant women. However, the first icon is unexpected.

What does this first icon tell us about Brazilian values? It looks like the obese are also given special consideration. Perhaps North American culture debates more whose fault it is for obesity. Is it a matter of eating well and exercising, or is it a

3.14 Lots of Help at the Concession Stand
We can assume that more workers means more personal attention, right?

matter of genetics? Perhaps Brazilians look at things differently. This photo is an excellent example of how much we can learn about Brazilian values by observing how society is put together. Thus, our second recommendation is to identify the values that are behind certain behaviors.

Third: Identify the Social Issues That Are Resolved by Things That Are Culturally Different

Social organization potentially reveals how a society resolves some of its problems. For example, in countries where few people can afford a car, the need for a developed mass transit system resolves the problem of how to move people around. Brazil is a country whose social organization reveals its approach to resolving some of its problems. An example of this is clearly seen in photo 3.14, where we see no fewer than ten people behind the counter at a concession stand at a sporting event. Chances are that this amount of work could be done by three or four people. As a foreigner, you may think that this is wasteful or terribly inefficient. However, this gives ten Brazilians a job to do. And furthermore, Brazilians focus a lot on the quality of personal attention that customers receive. More workers means that more people can receive personal attention. So our third recommendation is to identify the social issues that are resolved by things that are culturally different.

WRAPPING IT UP

When you interact with Brazilians, take time to truly interact with the people. Find a common group or interest—for example, soccer, music, religion, or education—and through it observe and learn more about Brazilians. Social organization, within the LESCANT approach, provides us with a way to observe these groups and how they might differ from our own.

SUMMARY OF BRAZILIAN SOCIAL ORGANIZATION

What we know about Brazil's social organization:

Kinship and family
- Taking care of those of the *terceiraidade* (third-age) "elderly."
- Deference to pregnant women, women with small children, the elderly, the disabled.
- A positive connotation for nepotism.

Education
- Fewer options for higher education.
- Taking the *cursinho* to prepare for the *vestibular.*
- *Ciênciasemfronteiras* (Science without Borders) to send thousands abroad to study.

Class system
- A new emerging middle class.
- The Brazilian "middle class" is not equivalent to the North American "middle class."

Gender roles
- A recognition of masculinity and femininity in professional matters.
- Sexual harassment and a hostile work environment are culturally defined.

Race
- A "postracial" society versus camouflaged racism.
- No designation for Hispanic or Latino.
- High percentages of the immigrant population are from Italy, Spain, Germany, Japan, Lebanon, and Syria.
- Indigenous groups come from hundreds of different tribes.

Individualism versus collectivism
- Brazilians have a collectivist, group mentality.
- The quality of life is improved for all when we focus on how groups can work together.

Religion
- Brazil is the largest Roman Catholic country in the world.
- It has a growing number of Protestants.
- It has high levels of syncretism.

Sports
- Many Brazilians are fitness-minded.
- Choose your soccer team.
- Brazilians focus more on the emotional side of sports than the analytical side.

Communication strategies on how to deal with Brazil's social organization:

- Be flexible in accepting organizational differences—begin with the premise that there must be a logical reason why people do what they do.
- Identify the values behind the behaviors.
- Identify what social issues are resolved by things that are culturally different.

4

BRAZILIAN
Contexting
I'll Call You, Really I Will

Navigating the subtleties in communication styles can be a challenge. Often, we rely on cues that we have learned over time. If you are in a completely new cultural environment, however, these same cues might not be there—or might be radically different. This chapter focuses on differences in contexting. "Contexting" is a specialized term, coined by Edward T. Hall to describe cultural differences in how directly or indirectly people communicate.[1] Hall set up a scale from low context, meaning explicit and direct, to high context, meaning implicit and indirect.

The United States is very low on the contexting scale; people tend to say what they really mean in blunt and direct terms. Brazil is much higher on the same scale; people tend to be much less direct. This difference in contexting is responsible for one of the most significant causes for cross-cultural misunderstanding between the two countries. When we deal with people from any culture that exhibits a higher context than our own, certain positive and negative features are predictable. Once we are aware of these features, we can cut through much of the cross-cultural conflict they cause.

Contexting is something that only exists in comparative terms. In other words, what matters is the difference between your own home culture and the culture that you are visiting. For example, Brazilians will seem to display a higher context to their North American counterparts because Brazil is higher on the context scale than the United States. At the same time, the same Brazilian who will seem to be high context in the United States will seem to be low context in Japan. This is because while Brazil shows higher context than the United States, it displays lower context than Japan. Similarly, a visitor from the United States who will seem to be low context in Brazil will seem to be high context in Germany. This is because while the United States is more low context than Brazil, it finds itself as more high context than Germany. In short, it is all relative. In a low-context culture such as the United States, what people say is what they mean. But in a high-context culture such as Brazil, people are less direct and expect others to interpret the meaning or, to use the American figure of speech, to "read between the lines" (figure 4.1).

First, let us look at how people from high-context cultures appear to those from low-context cultures. On the positive side, people from a more high-context culture than our own will strike us as being flexible, very polite, considerate, and able to anticipate our needs almost as if they were reading our minds. On the negative side, it will seem to us that the person from a more high-context culture is not quite honest, as if they are hiding something, possibly lying, or in any case being frustratingly vague. They will also seem inconsistent at best in how they follow rules, regulations, and procedures. This is how Brazilians usually seem to North Americans because Brazil is a more high-context culture in this case.

Now let us look at this the opposite way around. People from a low-context orientation (here, the United States) will exhibit certain characteristics to those from high-context cultures (here, Brazil). On the positive side, people from a more low-context culture than our own will strike us as being orderly, truthful, and very clear. On the negative side, it will seem to us that the

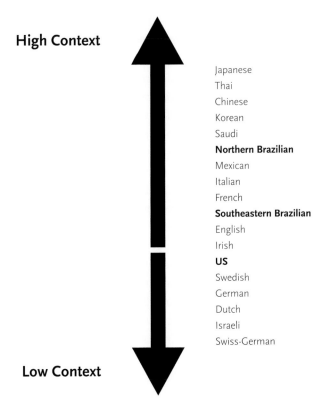

High Context

Japanese
Thai
Chinese
Korean
Saudi
Northern Brazilian
Mexican
Italian
French
Southeastern Brazilian
English
Irish
US
Swedish
German
Dutch
Israeli
Swiss-German

Low Context

Figure 4.1
Contexting Scale among Countries

person from a more low-context culture is rude and uncaring about anyone else's feelings, and is so unable to pick up on what is obvious to everyone else that they may seem dense. It will also seem that they are obsessed with following the rules to the point of absurdity. This is how most people from the United States usually seem to Brazilians because the United States is by comparison a more low-context culture in this case.

RULE ORIENTATION AND CONTEXTING

Contexting also extends beyond how people communicate with each other to include how cultures feel bound by formal rules.

In high-context cultures such as Brazil, people rely on context to determine appropriate behavior on a case-by-case basis. In low-context cultures, such as the United States, people are much more likely to rely on set rules to determine behavior.

How much we feel constrained by rules and regulations changes according to where we fall on the contexting scale. When a culture is higher than your own, that culture seems too lax when it comes to following the rules. When a culture is lower than your own, that culture seems too strict in following the rules. Before we go on, it might help to give some examples to review this concept; consider the following scenario:

> Suppose you are alone driving your car at 3 am in the morning and that you are stopped at a red light. There are no other cars or pedestrians in sight. There are no police-men or any other electronic surveillance nearby. Do you drive through the red light (because, after all, it does not make sense to simply sit there in this situation), or do you wait for the green light, even if that is a bit inconvenient (because, after all, in the end things work better when we all follow the laws)?

For those who drive through the red light, the situation of the moment determines their behavior (i.e., no cars, 3 am, no police, etc.). They are, in other words, high-context-oriented people because they consider the *context* of the situation over the mere rules. For those who wait for the green light, the rules determine their behavior, no matter what the situation of the moment may suggest. They are low-context-oriented people because the context of the situation is not as important as the basic rule.

Similar to how individuals differ in their tendency to prefer specific, written rules, or to look at the context of the moment, there are cultural norms that do the same. Generally, it is said that Brazilian culture, for example, displays more characteristics of a high-context behavior than the average North American does. (And we can add that when talking about traffic patterns in Brazil, Brazilians definitely believe that traffic rules are guidelines that have lots of flexibility based on the situation!)

Because low-context individuals do not consider the context of the moment as much, they depend more on actual rules, laws, and instructions. It is said that low-context individuals depend more on actual written and verbal communication. They want to specifically hear it or read it. It is for this reason that they appreciate it when other people specifically express their opinions with a clear "yes" or "no." High-context people consider the environment and their surroundings in order to determine a proper course of action. It is for this reason that high-context individuals need to gather more information, because they need more context.

WHAT DOES BEING DIRECT VERSUS BEING INDIRECT REALLY MEAN?

Cultures that are more low context than your own communicate more directly than you do. Cultures that are more high context than your own communicate more indirectly than you do. As members of a low-context culture, North Americans strike Brazilians as highly literal. When North Americans answer a question, they provide no context for it. Each question seems to be answered in a vacuum, with no thought to *why* or *how* that question was asked. At the same time, North Americans seem obsessed with getting "yes-or-no" answers. To Brazilians, they seem almost like the binary programming of a computer. For Brazilians, each situation depends on its context, on the relationship between the people involved, on the human element. Brazilians have a hard time understanding that their US counterparts do not seem to care about context. Because North Americans are more low context, they seem extraordinarily literal to Brazilians. North Americans take words at face value, placing great stress on *what* is said rather than *how* someone says those words. This is all very foreign to Brazilians.

As members of a high-context culture, Brazilians communicate more indirectly than their US counterparts. Brazilians accomplish this by learning as much about you as they can. By getting to know you, Brazilians can pick up what it means when you give someone a particular look. In fact, for Brazilians, *how* you say something matters more than *what* you have actually said. Brazilians remember what things you feel uncomfortable discussing or what subjects are likely to be difficult for you to understand. When Brazilians know that something is going to make you uncomfortable, they couch it in a way that makes it easier to hear. For instance, Brazilians will agree to do something that they have no intention of doing, just to be polite—but because you know each other so well, you already know by *how* they say "yes" that the real answer is "no."

Because Brazilians tend to say what the other person wants to hear (at least when put in US terms), they provide a lot of context for whatever they are saying so that you can determine what the real answer is. If you ask Brazilians a question, they will reply with an extensive explanation and perhaps never answer the question. If you were to demand a "yes-or-no" answer (which would feel quite rude to them), Brazilians would tell you "yes" (assuming that is what you want to hear). That "yes," however, is not the actual answer. The lengthy explanation—or, perhaps, the significant look—is your real answer. Over time, as your relationship builds, it becomes easier and easier to read each other because both of you are relying on *stored information* to communicate.

HOW CAN I GET A HANDLE ON ALL THIS?

If you are from a low-context culture, this may all seem a bit hard to follow at first. But there is a shortcut that you already know about. If you have a close relationship—with a parent, a spouse, or a partner—you already have a high-context relationship. If you have ever received "the look" and known something was wrong, you are already communicating in a high-context way through stored information. This is because any long-term, close relationship builds up context through stored information. This is the same for Brazilians or North Americans or for anyone else. The difference is that in high-context cultures, people also communicate this way outside these close personal relationships.

To illustrate this further, consider what happens when two people are out on a date for the first time. While driving to the restaurant, if there is silence in the car, that silence is extremely uncomfortable. Because the two people barely know each other, there are no shared experiences or shared context. For this reason, they need words. They need to hear actual conversation. Silence, in this instance, is extremely uncomfortable. However, compare this scenario with that of a couple that has been married for thirty years. That couple can drive down the road in total silence and total comfort. They have thirty years of shared experiences, and as such, there is no need to fill the silence. Consider further that when the couple that has been married for thirty years arrives at the restaurant, the husband might order chicken Alfredo for his wife, without even consulting her. It may be that in thirty years, he has learned that his wife's favorite food is chicken Alfredo, and this is the only dish she likes at this restaurant. Imagine, however, what it would mean if the guy on the first date ordered chicken Alfredo without consulting his date. The couple that has been married for thirty years simply has built more context than the couple out on the first date. In some ways, we might say that Brazilians act more like the couple that has been married for thirty years. They like to store information that can then be used at a later time. Similarly, North Americans are more similar to the couple that is out on a date for the first time. North Americans like to actually come out and state things directly, with less of a need to store information.

CONTEXTING VARIATIONS BY REGION AND OCCUPATION

Contexting varies not only between countries but often also between regions and even occupations within a country. In the United States, people in the northeastern states—and notably the area of Greater New York City, New Jersey, and eastern Pennsylvania—are more low context than people in the

Midwestern states. People in the Midwestern states, in turn, are notably more low context than people in the Deep South. Thus, even within a US context, we can hear comments (from people outside the region) such as "New Yorkers are rude, but at least you know where you stand" or "Alabamans are so polite, but sometimes you can't tell if they are putting you down or really mean what they've just said." These are reflections of contexting.

In Brazil, these regional contexting differences are much more pronounced than they are in the United States. As a rule, the farther north in Brazil you go, the higher-contexted the people will be. In the case of Brazil, the contexting differences between regions are wide enough to reflect almost another culture altogether. Thus, Brazilians in the Southeast of the country often have communication breakdowns with Brazilians in the North of the country that may be more pronounced than they would with some foreigners. As a result, Paulistas in the South and Recifenses in the North may both find it easier to understand foreigners from France than each other. This is because, on the contexting scale, France falls somewhere between southern and northern Brazil.

As an added point here, contexting varies a bit by occupation as well. Certain professions demand precise answers. Engineers, accountants, information systems professionals, and chemists, for example, tend to require a certain amount of specificity and directness. This makes the people in these fields seem more low context than others in their own culture.

Lawyers, advertising agents, public relations agents, and human resources managers, by contrast, tend to require a certain amount of sensitivity and finesse in much of what they communicate. This makes the people in these fields appear more high context than others in their own culture.

That said, even the lowest-contexted Brazilian engineer and the highest-contexted North American human resources manager work within their own national environment. Moreover, such occupational differences are much more likely in a professional setting than outside the workplace. See table 4.1 for a summary of Brazilian and North American contexting.

Table 4.1
Brazilian and North American Contexting Compared

High Context—Brazil	Low Context—North America
Great stress is placed on nonverbal messages; how a message is said matters more than what is said.	Great stress is placed on words and technical signs; what is said matters more than how it is said.
Fluid decision making, acting as a function of situations as they develop	Highly structured information for decision making
Authority through demonstrated behavior carries much respect.	Symbols of authority carry much respect.
Skeptical about advertising and propaganda	Vulnerable to advertising and propaganda
Decisions are given with extensive explanation.	Decisions are expected to be of the "yes/no" variety.

Note: These characterizations are derived, with modifications, from the work of Edward T. Hall, *The Silent Language* (Garden City, NY: Doubleday, 1959).

BRAZILIAN EXAMPLES OF A HIGH-CONTEXT CULTURE

Let us look at some examples, through photographs, of how Brazilians exemplify the characteristics of a high-context culture. You will find that Brazilians work hard to be polite, act with civility, and "save face" in situations where someone may become embarrassed. They are also tolerant when communication is more vague and when speech is less direct. We will see, by comparison, that North American culture demonstrates more characteristics of a low-context culture. North Americans rely more on the actual and literal words that are used to communicate. They give more attention to detail. They understand communications literally, and they appreciate direct communication styles. The chapter ends with some recommendations about how to deal with these differences when working with Brazilians, in situations where high-context and low-context styles come into play.

One of the characteristics of high-context communication is the need to provide more context. That is to say, instead of just giving rules or instructions, high-context communication requires adding the reasons for the rules and instructions. Let us look at some examples of this for Brazil.

Odebrecht is one of Latin America's largest engineering and construction companies. Photo 4.1 was taken at the construction site of the Corinthians' soccer stadium, where the opening game of the 2014 World Cup was played. The reminder to be safe—*Não se acidente* (Don't get in an accident)—is preceded by the statement *Você é muito importante para sua família* (You are very important to your family). Note also the illustration of a happy family with grandma, a chocolate cake, and the rest of the family. We see the extra information that reminds workers that it is not enough to be safe at work, but one should also seek to be safe because the family wants daddy to come home at the end of the day. This is a beautiful example of a rule that is enhanced with additional context.

To understand this second example, remember that the legal drinking age in Brazil is eighteen years of age. Whenever a Brazilian goes to the supermarket to buy alcohol, there is a good chance that in the beverage section, there will be a sign similar to the one in photo 4.2. If the sign were located in a culture that is more focused on low-context communication, it might simply state *Álcool para menores é proibido* (Alcohol to minors is

4.1 Don't Get in an Accident
Don't get in an accident, . . . because you are important to your family.

4.2 Alcohol Is Prohibited
Alcohol is prohibited, and we see all the reasons why!

prohibited). However, in a more high-context-oriented culture like Brazil, there is a tendency to explain why a rule is given. In this case we see the additional information *Bebida alcoólica pode causar dependência química e, em excesso, provoca graves males à saúde* (Alcoholic beverages can cause chemical dependence and, in excess, can cause serious harm to your health). Again, we see the rule, enhanced with additional information that provides a context for the rule.

In the third example (photo 4.3), a sign was posted in a public area in Rio de Janeiro. This is a no smoking symbol with the words *Rio sem fumo* (Rio without smoking). If Brazil were a low-context culture, that would be sufficient. But because Brazil is a more high-context culture, the sign adds extra background information: *Espaço ao ar livre é o que não falta. No Brasil, 7 pessoas morrem por dia por conta do tabagismo passivo. É coerente fumar neste ambiente? Se você é fumante, colabore* (Space in fresh air is not what is lacking. In Brazil 7 people die every day because of second-hand smoking. Is it fair to smoke in this area? If you are a smoker, collaborate). This sign happens to have six additional lines of explanatory background!

BRAZILIAN CONTEXTING

85

4.3 No Smoking Here
No smoking here, and we see all of the reasons why!

4.4 No Alcohol
No alcohol beyond this point. Period!

By way of comparison, photo 4.4 was taken in Austin, at the University of Texas Alumni Center. The sign simply says "No Alcohol Beyond This Point." Notice that there is no additional information, no description, no reasoning, not even a graphic illustration. This is typical of communication from a low-context orientation that simply gives the information with no additional background material.

Of course, we are not saying that in Brazil there are no signs that simply tell people the rule. Instead, we are saying that there is a tendency in Brazil to provide additional information that helps people understand the reason behind the rules.

Sometimes, communication in high-context cultures does the opposite of adding additional information. That is, sometimes things are stated in a way that only hints at the rule or that subtly suggests a behavior. The rules are not directly stated because there is an assumption that people understand the context surrounding the behavior. For example, photo 4.5 was taken at a restaurant in Santa Teresa in Rio de Janeiro. Almost every restaurant in Brazil has a sink for people to wash their hands before eating. The sign next to the sink in this restaurant simply states *Duas folhas secam suavemente as mãos* (Two sheets softly dry your hands). Notice that the instructions do not specifically tell users that they are only to use two sheets. This information is hinted at and suggested. There is no need to directly say "Only use two sheets!" High-context cultures are more apt to hint at instructions, because directly stating them is seen as too harsh and too blunt. Instructions are softened by simply hinting at the suggested behavior.

Here is another sign that hints at a behavior. Photo 4.6 was taken in front of a store in São Paulo that does not allow dogs inside. In a low-context culture, we are likely to simply see a sign that says "No dogs allowed." However, in Brazil the sign gives a much softer suggestion by merely saying *O lugar dele não é lá dentro* (His place is not inside). Notice that it does not come out and specifically say that dogs are not allowed, but without being too blunt, we all get the hint.

4.5 Use Only Two Paper Towels
Just hinting that one should only use two sheets to dry your hands.

4.6 A Dog's Place
"No dogs allowed" versus "His place is not inside."

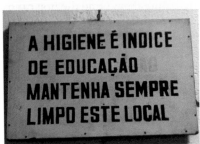

4.7 Keep It Clean
"Hygiene is a sign of education," meaning "Keep it clean here!"

Photo 4.7 again hints at proper behavior. This sign was posted on the wall of a restaurant in São Paulo. The sign reads *A higiene é índice de educação. Mantenha sempre limpo este local* (Hygiene is a sign of education. Always keep this place clean). The implication here is that polite people will get the hint and do their best to keep the place clean. Notice again that the management is giving instructions to the customers, but the wording is specifically soft, avoiding the bold directness of a command.

When experts talk about the characteristics of low-context communication, they usually center on the fact that low-context cultures give information directly, put things in writing, or say things specifically in words. Be careful, however. Notice that the examples from the photographs above have focused on the extra background information that is given. There is a difference. Low-context cultures provide instructions in order to tell people *what* they should do. In high-context cultures, people provide additional information that explains *why* the instructions should be followed.

To illustrate this difference, the photos 4.8 and 4.9 were taken on subways, one in Philadelphia and the other in São Paulo. The photograph from the Philadelphia subway gives riders a long and detailed list of what is permitted on the trains. None of this information tells the riders the reason for the rules. There is simply a long list of rules—for example, cell phones cannot be used, text messaging must be on vibrate or mute, earphones must be used, conversations should be short and conducted in a whisper, electronic devices must be placed on vibrate, and the first car of each train is designated as the QuietRide car. This is an excellent example of low-context communication that provides detailed rules, but no extra background reasons or explanations.

Compare the QuietRide photo with the next one from the São Paulo subway that encourages riders to be courteous, *Faça um grande gesto* (Do a nice gesture). Riders then are given the rule *Dê passagem para quem sai do trem* (Give way to those who are leaving the train). If Brazil were a low-context culture, that is where the instructions would end. However, as members of a high-context culture, riders are then given a long explanation as to why they should give way to others: *Um simples gesto faz uma grande diferença. O metro é feito de milhões de pessoas, milhões de gestos. Dê o seu melhor e ajude a construir o Metrô que você quer. O metro fica melhor com você* (A simple gesture makes a big difference. The Metro is made up of millions of people, millions of gestures. Give your best and help make the Metro what you want it to be. The Metro is better with you.) Unlike the Philadelphia train, the São Paulo train does not simply give rules, but also focuses on giving more background information and context to help riders understand why they should follow the rules.

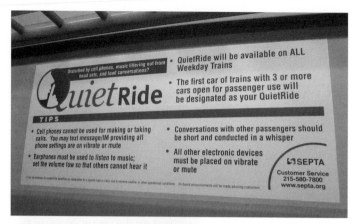

4.8 QuietRide
List of what the rules are for the trains in Philadelphia. © John Corbet. Used by permission.

4.9 Make a Nice Gesture
List of why we should obey the rules in the subway in São Paulo.

HOW TO USE WHAT YOU KNOW ABOUT CONTEXTING TO ENCOURAGE GOOD COMMUNICATION

Navigating contexting differences can be challenging because generally we are unaware of how we communicate. Yet if you start paying attention to the cues around you, it is something that will begin to pop out. To get you started, we offer the following recommendations related to how to deal with Brazilians.

Direct versus Indirect Communication Styles

To a Brazilian, the direct speaking style that is typical of low-context communicators comes across as sounding extremely blunt and harsh. When, for example, North Americans say things like "I think Carlos is lazy" or "I hate kids" or "I want this on my desk by 9 o'clock sharp" all these sentences sound extremely bold. Brazilians are not sure how to respond to such direct declarations. Be aware of this, and try to soften some of these statements.

Brazilians work hard to make people feel good, which, to low-context communicators, sounds evasive. Brazilians do not like to give bad news and will do all they can to avoid directly saying something negative. For example, if a Brazilian is invited to do something that he or she does not want to do, a typical response will be something like *Vou pensar* (I'll think about it) or *Te ligo* (I'll give you a call) or *Se Deus quiser* (God willing) or *Se não chover* (if it does not rain). In other words, they will not come out and say "no." Instead, they will give a noncommitted response that leaves things open. Basically, the other party is supposed to get the hint that the answer is no. The problem is that sometimes low-context communicators do not get the hint.

It is not hard to imagine a situation where a North American is trying to sell something to a Brazilian, who in reality is not interested in buying. The Brazilian has given every hint that she is not interested; but unfortunately, because the North American has not specifically heard "I do not want to buy this," he holds out hope that maybe there is still a chance. The poor Brazilian must be thinking "What do I need to do to get this guy to understand that I do not want to buy his product?"

Do Not Take Every Comment So Literally

A similar and related problem also exists, and that is when low-context people interpret what Brazilians say literally, even though the Brazilians did not attach the literal meaning to their words. For example, if a Brazilian invites someone to dinner, that invitation may just be a social nicety, without any real intent to actually go out to dinner. A Brazilian would respond to the invitation by saying something like how nice a dinner together would be someday. If the invitation is genuine, then it will be pushed a little more, and at some point a real follow-up will take place. If the invitation was just a social nicety, then it will always be something both realize is talked about as a possibility for some other day. The problem for low-context communicators is that they will pull out their calendar and try to schedule the exact time for the dinner, which may not have been an actual invitation. Our recommendation is that you do not hold Brazilians to every word that they say. The intent is more important than the actual words.

We recently had an experience in Brazil that reminded us of this issue. While in Salvador, we had some problems with our apartment. Our landlord told us that he would swing by "tomorrow morning" to take a look at things. We modified our schedule to make sure that we would be at home in the morning. Not only did the landlord not come by the apartment that morning, but it was three days later when he finally did come over. When he arrived, he offered no excuse or apology for being late. In fact, we are sure that he had no concept that he had specifically said that he would come "tomorrow morning." We, however, had made the mistake of interpreting his words literally.

The Takeaway

Our recommendation is that those from low-context cultures be sensitive to how blunt you may sound to Brazilians. They are caught off guard by such direct communication. North Americans are well known for their summarized, streamlined, and executive-summary approach communication. However, this constant need for summaries and outlines can be perceived as an oversimplification of communication, especially among people who believe that details matter. Do not be too quick to summarize everything into brief bullet points. Second, be aware that Brazilians will try hard not to give negative information. Take the hint, and follow suit. Read between the lines to capture when someone is not willing or when someone disagrees. And finally, do not hold Brazilians to specific words and phrases that they say. Often those statements were not pronounced with the same literal interpretation that you think they had.

It Takes Time to Build Context

Because Brazilians come from a more high-context starting point in their communication, do not be surprised if they spend a lot of time learning extra details about their potential working partners. If Brazilians spend hours showing you around town, taking you out to see the local sights, or sit around a restaurant table for extremely long dinners, realize that all this is simply a matter of adding context to your relationship. If you find yourself thinking that everyone is wasting time instead of getting down to "real" work, then chances are that you are working with a Brazilian who needs to build more context into the relationship. Brazilians need to know if their working partner likes sports, enjoys beaches, prefers wine, likes cold beer, reads novels, understands politics, or loves to hear about historical facts and figures. The more we know of a person, the more context we can create, and the better we can respond to that person's needs. This is how Brazilians look at working relationships. Of course, this does not apply to every Brazilian and every instance, but it is common to deal with people who simply need time to build the context.

We have met North Americans who, when engaging with Brazilians, do not realize the importance of giving time for the building of context. For example, it is not uncommon for Brazilians to bring up the topic of soccer. We have witnessed North Americans who say such things as "I hate soccer; what a boring game." Talk about a conversation killer! Soccer is not what is important here; what is important is the need to connect with another person. We recommend that all North American visitors would do well to choose a soccer club as "your" team, and then you can be part of the whole soccer conversation. Give context building its time.

In giving time for context building, Brazilians also go out of their way to be helpful to others. Part of this help includes involving other people in the process. For example, if you are looking for an address or a building, do not be surprised if Brazilians start asking strangers on the street, taxi drivers who drive by, or friends in the back room to help out. A low-context person will be focusing on the information, and will expect a person to simply state whether he or she knows the information or not. But that is not the Brazilian way. Brazilians will involve others in the process because, in their minds, it is not just the information that is important; it is also the fact that a person needs that information from them. It is as if Brazilians are thinking "Some day I might need help from this person. If I help her now, someday she may be able to help me too." We have seen North Americans who get frustrated with Brazilians who are trying to help them, even when those Brazilians really do not know what to do. Relax. Brazilians go out of their way to help because they see this as a way to build a better connection, for future opportunities that may arise.

Do Not Trap Brazilians in a Corner

Because low-context communicators are most comfortable hearing the actual words that are spoken, there is a tendency to resolve issues by asking to hear specific statements. This is quite typical of North America, for example, where people like to know where they stand. If a person is not interested in buying a product, a North American would like to wrap things up with a firm response like "No thank you, I am not interested in buying your product." Similarly, if a North American does not have information that is asked for, there is nothing wrong in simply stating "Sorry, I do not know the answer to your question."

Individuals from cultures that have a more high-context style of communication are more sensitive to not embarrassing others. The focus is not on the information; it is on the person who conveys the information. It is for this reason that there is a greater effort exerted in helping someone preserve his or her dignity or to not lose face. This is why if Brazilians are not interested in something, or if they do not know the answer, they are more cautious in how they express it. A Brazilian does not want to embarrass himself or herself, or the other person.

Our recommendation is that we do not force Brazilians to explicitly say something that is already understood. If everyone knows that the answer is no, then do not make them say it out loud. Do not force them into a corner. By forcing them to say things out loud, we are not only making them feel uncomfortable, but we are also not allowing them to save face or prevent embarrassment. What might be a little embarrassing to a

North American will be a stronger attack on a person's dignity in Brazil. If they are wrong, they know it. Nothing is accomplished by forcing them to explicitly state what is already known tacitly. When a Brazilian stops returning phone calls, no longer answers e-mails, gives evasive answers, or makes excuses, the best recourse is to simply take the hint and to realize that he or she is trying to softly tell you "no."

Contexting Varies within Brazil

Keep in mind that the farther north you go, the more all these differences grow. This is the case not only between North Americans and Brazilians but also between Brazilians from south to north as well. Also keep in mind that some contexting differences occur according to the nature of each profession. That said, even when the lowest-contexted Brazilian engineer and the highest-contexted North American human resources manager interact, a significant contexting gap will still remain.

WRAPPING IT UP

The issue of contexting is one of those where the more we understand the difference between low-context and high-context communication, the more we see examples of it in daily life. We can almost guarantee that as you observe Brazilian exchanges, you will come away with hundreds of examples that exemplify their need to add context to the communication.

SUMMARY OF BRAZILIAN CONTEXTING

What we know about Brazil's contexting:

Context defined
- Communication that depends on actual words that are spoken (or written) is thought of as low context.
- Communication that depends on previously obtained information (i.e., context) is thought of as high context.

Brazilian and North American contexting
- Brazilian communication is more high context than typical North American communication.

Rule orientation and contexting
- Brazilians, who are more high context, allow the situation to define the appropriate behavior.
- North Americans, who are more low context, allow the rule to define appropriate behavior.

Implicit versus explicit communication
- As members of a high-context culture, Brazilians are more implicit in their speech, giving more attention to how something is said.
- As members of a low-context culture, North Americans are more explicit in stating things directly and literally, also with a specific yes or no.

Regional and occupational variations
- As a general rule, those from the northern regions of Brazil exhibit characteristics of being even more high context than those from the southern parts of the country.
- Another general rule: jobs that require precision exhibit more low-context communication, and jobs that require sensitivity and finesse require more high-context communication.

Communication strategies on how to deal with Brazil's contexting:

- Direct versus indirect communication styles
  - Do not take a Brazilian's comments too literally.
  - Do not force a Brazilian to come out and specifically say what he or she is hinting at. Take the hint.
  - Be sensitive to how blunt, direct, and bold a North American will sound to a Brazilian.
  - Be aware that a North American's tendency to summarize, streamline, and outline may be perceived as oversimplification.
- It takes time to build a relationship.
  - If you feel like you are wasting your time with social niceties and chit-chat, give it time.
  - If Brazilians seem overly helpful, it is evidence that they are building relationships.
- Do not trap Brazilians in a corner.
  - Brazilians are sensitive to not embarrassing others.
  - Brazilians work to preserve dignity and not lose face.
- Do not force them to explicitly state what is known tacitly.

5

BRAZILIAN
Authority
Conception

Show Me Some of That Jeitinho

We now turn our attention to the role of authority and power in intercultural communication: how we define power and authority, who has power, and how power is shared or exchanged. When we talk about authority, issues of leadership style, how decisions are made, and how titles are used to show status are also part of the conversation. Many of the issues related to authority are culturally based, which in this instance means that we need to understand how authority and power are perceived among Brazilians and how they address the problems they see.

Let us begin with a brief look at Brazilian government and politics, in both the role of government and the role of the political leaders. Brazil is a large country, in area, population, economy, and resources. As such, those who hold positions of authority receive the credit when things go well and receive blame when they do not. Brazil is a country with many laws, a complex tax structure, and issues related to corruption that all affect business interactions. Next, we take a look at how Brazil responds to outside authority and foreign presence. We then briefly look at authority and corruption. In a small section on how Brazilians have been responding to recent social problems, we focus on power and authority in this context. Then we look at the Brazilian *malandro* (which is defined below), a motif of sorts that exemplifies how Brazilians function in the absence of official power and authority. And this is followed by a discussion of *coronelismo* (again, defined below) to show how Brazilian culture relies on others to help open doors for opportunities. We also present a number of photographs that show power and authority in Brazil. Finally, we end the chapter with a number of recommendations related to intercultural communication with Brazilians, in light of authority and power.

STARTING AT THE TOP:
GOVERNMENT AND AUTHORITY

Our purpose here is not to give a complete essay on Brazilian government and politics, but simply to show how the country's authority is organized. This will give you a good framework for understanding Brazilians' approaches to power and authority. Thus, we limit ourselves to a brief description, focusing on issues that affect intercultural communication.

Governments have sovereignty, which brings up issues of autonomy, independence, freedom, power, and control. Like many countries in Latin America, Brazil's sovereignty has been tied to a struggle to balance the desire to be independent on one hand, building the quality of life for its own citizens, but on the other hand to be subordinate to the needs of others that have power over you. Historically, Brazil has generally relied on exports. From its beginnings in the colonial era, Brazil started with the necessity to export sugarcane, coffee, gold, precious stones, and raw materials. Even the name of the country refers back to *pau brasil*, a wood similar to mahogany that was exported to Europe. All the aspects of Brazil's growth—including the exploration and expansion along the coast, the adoption of the slave trade from Africa, and the push for immigrants from countries as diverse as Japan and Italy—were motivated by the need for exportation.

As is the case with many other Latin American nations, Brazil today still struggles with the thought that this historical emphasis (some would argue *over*emphasis) on exports has hampered the development of its citizens at home. As a result, the Brazilian government seems confusing from an outside perspective—and even to many Brazilians. One reason is that Brazilian laws, tax structure, policies, and attitudes about governance are often inconsistent and even contradictory. How did this happen? Brazil, as a government, must continually try to balance the global demands of an export-driven economy with a domestic desire to shift power back to its own citizens. Brazil is happy to collaborate with foreigners, but there must be a perceived benefit for Brazilians. If people view foreign collaboration as having as its only goal the exporting of Brazil's products and services for its business sector, or—worse yet—the perceived exploitation of Brazil, then Brazilians are not willing to participate. Foreigners who interact or do business with Brazil will benefit from an understanding of these issues.

The Export Globalists versus the Populists

The reason that foreigners need to be concerned to balance economic benefit with serving the needs of the general population stems from a very divisive and ongoing debate in Brazilian politics between global free market elements and nationalist populist elements. Indeed, much of Brazil's economic and political history of the last one hundred years has consequently seemed to follow a pendulum's course, swinging back and forth between the two opposite sides of this debate.

On one side, we have what we can call the export globalists. The globalists represent Brazil's traditional export-driven interests (i.e., exports) and the attendant need for Brazil to be actively involved as part of an integrated world economy (globalists). On the other side, we have what we can call the nationalist populist interests. The nationalist populists represent Brazil's attempt to act independent of outside interference (nationalists) and to serve the needs of the underserved masses (populists).

Brazil's export globalists see the country's dependence on foreign markets as the engine of its economy that has served as the source of its prosperity since colonial times. Those favoring these export-driven interests see Brazil's development and prosperity as depending at least in part on the involvement of foreigners in Brazil, through foreign direct investment and the dictates of a free market economy. They see as positive the fact that consumers determine what and how much Brazil produces. Because Brazil depends heavily on exports, these export globalists view the demands of consumers buying Brazilian products abroad not as foreign interference in Brazil's affairs but as no different than the demands of Brazil's own domestic consumers.

The other side of this political spectrum is the nationalist populists' position. Their goals can be summarized as economic independence, political sovereignty, and economic justice. For these nationalist populists, it is important to have Brazil's economy be determined by Brazilian needs (economic independence) rather than foreign consumers' needs. To achieve this goal, its proponents support a policy that economists call "Latin American structuralism." This name reflects the fact that this approach has an appeal that goes far beyond just Brazil, with Argentina (where it is a central tenet of the political movement called Peronism) as its strongest advocate. Latin American structuralism in Brazil promotes a policy called *substituição de importações* (import substitution), whereby the government creates industry to eliminate dependence on foreign sources. In principle, the *substituição de importações* policy makes Brazil independent of the need to import products and allows Brazil to become less reliant on exports as its need to balance the cost of imports disappears. This, in turn, achieves the national sovereignty goal that allows Brazil to avoid dependence on (or, as some see it, to avoid being controlled by) foreign influences (nationalists). The final part of the argument is that once Brazil becomes economically independent and free of foreign influences, the country can better the lot of its poor and serve the needs of its people.

What we have just described is how each of these sides views itself. That said, both sides of this debate, however, view each other in very different ways. The export globalists see the policies of nationalist populism as irresponsibly creating unfunded mandates. They view the nationalist populist approach as spending for infrastructure building and social services without having the money to pay for them. By contrast, those favoring nationalist populism view their initiatives as serving the needs of the people. And those favoring nationalist populism see the export-driven interests as allowing their government to be run by outsiders and the country's prosperity as benefiting only an elite minority while the needs of common citizens remain unmet.

AN OVERVIEW OF RECENT BRAZILIAN POLITICS

These export globalist and nationalist populist views are more than theory. Politicians on both sides have had substantial periods in power in recent years. To get a feel for this, it is probably necessary to give a brief overview of Brazilian policies from the height of the nationalist populists' success under Juscelino Kubitschek (who was elected in 1956) to the Brazilian economic upheavals of the "lost decades" of the 1970s and 1980s and the export globalists' policies, which have been in place from 1995 until today.

This is a historically interesting period because it so clearly shows how the pendulum has swung between these two policies. From the 1950s through 1969, the nationalist populists largely governed Brazil under both elected and military governments. The inspiring high point of the nationalist populist approach came with the development and construction of Brasilia as the capital city of Brazil. Focusing inward, Brazil moved its capital from Rio de Janeiro to an uninhabited location in what was then only jungle. In doing so, Brazil created a symbol of the nationalist populist dream of a new Brazil, modern in its focus and uninfluenced by outside sources. That was in 1960, under the presidential leadership of Juscelino Kubitschek. The cost of Brasilia, however, was high, and the country had difficulty paying for it. As a result, the Brazilian economy faltered. Still, the nationalist populists' approach held sway for subsequent decades. They maintained power when, four years later, the Brazilian military forces overthrew President João Goulart in the 1964 coup d'état. A military regime ruled Brazil for the next twenty years. Populism's hold actually increased as a policy position when civilian government was reinstated in 1985. In short, from 1974 to 1995 nationalist populism remained the Brazilian position, whether under military dictatorships or, after 1985, for the first decade under civilian-elected governments.

Populism was only briefly interrupted from 1969 through 1973, when the military dictator Emílio Garrastazu Médici created an economic boom in Brazil by mixing the two approaches together, allowing Brazil to open more to the world economy. He did this by instituting an export globalist policy mixed with intense Brazilian nationalism. Proponents of export globalism—despite Médici's intense nationalism, which they oppose—call this period the *Milagre econômico brasileiro* (Brazilian economic miracle). At the same time, the nationalist populists—despite Médici's intense nationalism, which they favor—call the same era the *anos de chumbo* (years of lead).

Following the oil shocks of the 1970s, however, the nationalist populist policies could no longer sustain themselves. It took the almost total collapse of Brazil's economy to dislodge the nationalist populists' hold on the country. By the time Fernando Collor became president in 1989, Brazil's annual inflation rate had passed 1,500 percent. You read that right. When Collor resigned in 1992, following an impeachment vote of 441 to 38, the country shifted sharply to the export globalist approach, which was personified by the United States–educated Fernando Henrique Cardoso, who won the presidency in 1994.

Under Fernando Henrique's Plano Real, Brazil restructured its debt and committed itself to a firmly global and export-driven policy. Large-scale privatization of state-owned industry and measures to increase foreign investment stabilized the economy, and inflation fell to under 5 percent in fewer than two years. Brazil became so stable that even as the rest of Latin America was collapsing under the effect of the 1995 Mexican peso crisis, Brazil continued to grow. In fact, by 1996, Brazil ranked second only to China in foreign investment, receiving $26 billion in 1996 alone.

When the far-left Workers' Party candidate Luiz Inácio Lula da Silva (known universally as "Lula") became president in 2003, most observers both inside and outside Brazil expected the pendulum to swing back to the nationalist populist policy. It did not. Instead, Lula and his successor, Dilma Rousseff, left intact the export globalist policies of foreign direct investment and export-driven growth determined by free market forces inside and outside Brazil. In the end, Lula (and Rousseff after him) built on the foundation of Henrique's Plano Real, and introduced new social programs like Bolsa Família (Family Allowance) and Fome Zero (Zero Hunger) that focused on providing funding for lower-income families. In this way, since 2003, Brazil has focused much of its efforts on the populist goals of raising the standard of living and mean per capita income of Brazil's poor. In short, for a little over a decade, Brazil has seemingly kept the pendulum from swinging, in a sort of compromise between the two views. The result has been that since 1995, Brazil's middle class has continued to grow, and there is every reason to expect that it will continue to do so.

With Brazil in the limelight as it prepared to host the World Cup and Olympic games, the pendulum appeared to start swaying again. The export globalist approach began receiving sustained criticism as economic growth showed signs of slowing down and inflation rates threatened to go up. At the same time, the nationalist populists grew in strength. As the rate of improvements in the economy slowed, nationalist populists began to argue that building infrastructure for the World Cup and Olympics was benefiting foreigners and the wealthy elite more than average Brazilians. Many Brazilians resented the construction of these highly visible sports venues without similarly visible improvement in education, health care, roads, transportation, and public safety. This was exacerbated by evidence of government corruption in the construction of sports venues (and, presumably, in the failure to provide comparable levels of support for infrastructure for the common people). By mid-2013 protesters were taking to the streets. As the World Cup began in 2014, the country was facing the reality that much of the progress that was expected from infrastructure development was simply not happening, just as the nationalist populists have always argued. At the same time, because of the rapid growth of the middle class, arguably more Brazilians than at any time before have accepted (at least in part) the reality that Brazil's prosperity depends on participating in an integrated world economy, just as the export globalists have always argued. Thus, the decades-old conflict between nationalist populists and export globalists has come once again to the forefront. At the time of this writing, however, it is difficult to predict which way the pendulum will swing. Brazil has been shocked by a corruption scandal that involves Brazil's largest company, the state-run oil giant Petrobras. Massive kickbacks and money laundering have not only implicated officials at Petrobras, but even more damaging, embroiled a host of key leaders from many political parties. Brazilians find themselves in the difficult position of having to deal with effects of the scandal while at the same time grappling with a severe recession and increased inflation. The result has been intense polarization and division, both among Brazilians as well as others abroad. Stay tuned!

HOW BRAZIL'S LAWS DEMONSTRATE ITS VIEW OF OUTSIDE AUTHORITY

How does all this relate to intercultural communication and the issue of authority? The answer is that it provides a context for understanding why Brazil has some of the policies it does. For example, multinational companies doing business in Brazil discover that Brazilian law requires that the majority of the labor and the majority of the materials be Brazilian. These laws exist to promote Brazilian growth, and they stem from the feeling that, historically, Brazil has been exploited by outsiders. When multinational companies propose to build factories in Brazil, the first question they are asked is whether the company plans on staying in Brazil for a long time. If there is a sense that the multinational company is just out for quick, short-term profits, then Brazil is less interested in such a venture. This is also the reason why non-Brazilian companies face such high taxes to do business in Brazil. It all stems from the perception that Brazil should no longer be exploited by outside influences.

The result is that Brazil has cumbersome laws that add complexity to doing business in the country. Data from the World Bank indicate that it takes 108 days to start a business in Brazil.[1] What is particularly amazing is that this ranking is an *improvement* over earlier years (in 2009, it took 119 days to start a business!). Improvements notwithstanding, Brazil ranks fourth worst among all nations in business starting time. By comparison, among Brazil's fellow BRIC countries (i.e., Brazil, Russia, India, and China—the world's largest fast-growing economies), China takes 33 days, India takes 27, and Russia takes 15. Only Venezuela, Equatorial Guinea, and Suriname take more time. Within the Latin American context, Chile, Mexico, Panama, and Puerto Rico each take only 6 days to start a business. In the United States and Canada, similarly, it takes 5 days to start a business.

The Doing Business project of the World Bank also provides comparative data on the ease of doing business by country.[2] Brazil ranks 116 out of 189. This rank is based on such items as the time it takes to start a business, dealing with construction permits, getting electricity, registering property, getting credit, protecting investors, paying taxes, trading across borders, enforcing contracts, and resolving insolvency. Brazil ranks particularly low in the time it takes to start a business (123 out of 189) and also low in paying taxes (159 out of 189). In fact, the total tax rate (percentage profit) in Brazil is 68.3 percent. By comparison, the average in Latin America is 47.3 percent and the average for the countries that belong to the Organization for Economic Cooperation and Development is 41.3 percent. The bottom line is that it is difficult to start a business in Brazil, it is difficult to do business in Brazil, and it costs more in taxes to do business in Brazil.

We have an excellent example of the implications of these laws and regulations for foreign businesses. We know of a multinational company in the petroleum industry that has a factory in Brazil. The product that they build in Brazil has more than 1,000 parts, and currently some of these parts are manufactured in Singapore. The company looked into the possibility of moving this additional factory to Brazil, to be able to build these parts with Brazilian labor and to use Brazilian materials. Unfortunately, the tax rates that it would have to pay would make it more expensive to produce the parts in Brazil than in Singapore and to ship them to Brazil. It is these sorts of issues that confront multinational companies that hope to do business in Brazil.

AUTHORITY AND CORRUPTION

Another aspect of authority that affects operations in Brazil is the amount of corruption that exists in government and business. The truth is that the corruption index for Brazil is less than for many other countries. In 2013 Transparency International ranked Brazil 72 out of 177; the higher the numerical ranking, the worse the perception of corruption.[3] Denmark, for example, is perceived as the least corrupt, at 1 out of 177; and Somalia, North Korea, and Afghanistan tie for the most corrupt, at 175 out of 177. In Latin America only Chile and Uruguay are perceived as being less corrupt than Brazil. Moreover, Brazil has improved remarkably over the last several decades. When Fernando Henrique Cardoso won the presidency in 1995, Transparency International ranked Brazil as the fourth most corrupt nation in the world, with a score of only 2.70 out of a possible 10. In Latin America, Brazil was only slightly edged out by the 2.66 score of Venezuela—traditionally the region's most corrupt nation. Nor was such corruption a given throughout Latin America at that time. That same year, for instance, Argentina ranked 23rd, with a score of 5.24, and Chile, at 7.94, ranked 13th, which was actually less corrupt than the 14th-place United States, at 7.79. That same year, Canada was ranked the 5th cleanest, at 8.87, and New Zealand as least corrupt, at 9.55.

Despite the great strides Brazil has made in the last two decades in this regard, corruption has a cost. It also affects the perceptions of government, of its leaders, and of those in positions of power. Data from the Federação das Indústrias do Estado de São Paulo estimate that the annual cost of corruption in Brazil is between 1.38 percent and 2.3 percent of the country's total gross domestic product. If so, the cost of corruption in Brazil could be as high as $53 billion per year.[4] If this same amount of money were invested—for example, in sanitation—it would provide 23.3 million additional households with public sewer systems. Corruption has a cost.

An interesting example of corruption happened in Rio de Janeiro back in 2013, when six steel beams were removed from the *elevado da perimetral*, a raised portion of the highway that runs through the port area of Rio, between the airport and the south zone. The beams were set aside during the demolition of the highway, and then mysteriously six steel beams disappeared. Each beam was about 130 feet long, and each weighed more than 20 tons. And yet, mysteriously, somehow somebody had the capacity, expertise, and know-how to use cranes to lift the beams into trucks and make off with the beams. Some have called this theft the largest in the history of Brazil, at least in terms of weight and size. The beams were made of specially treated corrosive resistant steel that was valued at $660,000 (R$1.5 million). This story made the rounds for months in Brazil, always emphasizing that somebody had to know of the whereabouts of these beams, given the special and technical skills that would be required to remove them. As far as we know, the mystery was never solved.[5]

PUBLIC RESPONSE TO POWER AND AUTHORITY

As mentioned above, Brazil has experienced a new wave of public response, protesting the effects and abuses of those in authority. This new social activity has emerged in part because more people are aware of the social and economic inequalities in the country. The growing middle class has also increased the number of people who believe that they have a right to better social services. Another reason is that the country had high expectations about the benefits that the World Cup and Olympics would bring to Brazil's development and infrastructure. But those expectations did not match the actual changes that came about, and this also coincided with increased attention being given to government corruption.

At about this same time, in 2014, Fiat launched a promotional campaign that included a song titled "Vem pra rua" (Come to the Streets), performed by the popular rapper Falção. The catchy tune became the theme song for the protest:

> *Vem, vamos pra rua* (Come, let's go to the streets)
> *Pode vir que a festa é sua* (You can come cuz the party is yours)
> *Que o Brasil vai estar gigante* (Cuz Brazil is going to be gigantic)
> *Grande como nunca se viu* (Gigantic like you have never seen)

And the chorus adds,

> *Vem pra rua* (Come to the streets)
> *Porque a rua é a maior arquibancada do Brasil* (Cuz the streets are Brazil's largest grandstand)

Thousands of protesters hit the streets in dozens of cities all over the country. At the time Brazil was busy building new soccer stadiums in preparation for the 2014 World Cup. Reports of the excessive cost of the stadiums, together with accusations of corruption, only added to the protests against the political climate, the country's health policies, problems with education, issues about public transportation, and concerns regarding public security. One of our favorite protest posters declared "Desculpe o transtorno. Estamos mudando o Brasil" (Excuse the mess. We are changing Brazil). With all the construction and building projects that were being pursued in Brazil at the time, it was very common to see construction road signs that said "Desculpe o transtorno. Estamos em obras" (Excuse the mess. We are making repairs). The protest posters displayed a nice play on words, based on the construction signs.

Brazilians are actually accustomed to protests and strikes. In fact, there is generally a high tolerance for the inconveniences of strikes, and it is not uncommon for universities to experience teacher and staff strikes. Bank employees, security workers,

5.1 Strike, Brazilian Style
There is nothing like a strike to bring on a good party atmosphere!

police forces, public servants—they all frequently go on strike in Brazil. Generally, the public goes with the flow, adjusting travel and schedules to accommodate, and things move on without too much hassle. We have witnessed the violence of strikes in Brazil, but we have also witnessed the casualness and almost party-like atmosphere of other strikes. Photo 5.1 shows a group of strikers in São Paulo, on Avenida Paulista. All the banks were closed as part of this strike. The truth is that it was more of a Carnaval atmosphere, complete with costumes, wigs, samba music, and dancing, with lots of kisses and hugs among total strangers. Brazil is truly a country that has a high tolerance for the inconveniences of strikes. At the same time, admittedly, patience is wearing thin. The current corruption scandals have led to more violent protests and ugly demonstrations.

MALANDRO

In a society where few have real authority and power, people need to know how to work around that. One of the most popular expressions in Brazil is *dar um jeito*, which has a meaning similar to "finagle" or "manipulate." If the law says that something cannot be done, well, we need to *dar um jeito* to get it down. If the roads are blocked up, we need to *dar um jeito* to find a new way to arrive at our destination. Brazil is a country where *dar um jeito* is a way of life.

Brazilians also have another expression, *Há leis que pegam e leis que não pegam* (Some laws stick and other laws do not stick). Clever people deal with the complexities of authority by knowing which laws are enforced and which ones are ignored. Brazil is simply a country where people need to know how to get around, make exceptions, look for alternative ways to do something, and find influential people who can help along the way.

This is where the Brazilian *malandro* enters the picture. A dictionary translation of *malandro* might be "swindler" or "scoundrel." However, in Portuguese the word has as much of a positive connotation as a negative one. Perhaps a more appropriate translation would be "someone who is streetwise." A *malandro* is a person who has a strategy to gain an advantage in any given situation. The Walt Disney animated character Zê Carioca is clearly a character built on the stereotype of a *malandro*. *The malandro* enjoys a life of fun and pleasure, always has his wits about him, looks for the easy way out, manipulates people, and figures out a way to get what he wants. In fact, in Brazil people refer to a Lei de Gérson (Gerson's Law): *Gosto de levar vantagem em tudo* (I like to take advantage in everything). Gerson was a famous soccer player who made a television commercial in which he mentioned how he was always looking for the advantage in everything. The slogan stuck, because it resonated with the need to be a *malandro*.

The *malandro* is deemed necessary because Brazilian culture is extremely bureaucratic. Legal processes are long and slow, and the paperwork is suffocating. There is a lack of trust in the system. Anyone who needs to go to a Notary Office (Cartório do Brasil) knows that the process will take all day. In fact, in Brazil there are *despachantes* (brokers) who take care of all the paperwork. You cannot survive in Brazil without a good *despachante*. Truly, a *malandro* is a person who can work around the system when official authority gets in the way.

When considering the authority conception in Brazil, it helps to understand a leadership style that is known as *coronelismo*. Similar to *malandro, coronelismo* refers to the relationship where a person of influence (boss, government bureaucrat, et al.) has a variety of "clients" on whom he or she bestows favors. These favors are granted less in the form of material goods and more in removing obstacles. The *coronel*, for example, can speed up the process of obtaining necessary permits or secure job interviews for others. In return, the clients give undiluted loyalty to the *coronel*, who then is in a stronger position to call on others to remove even more obstacles.

This form of authority conception, which is not easy to see, is not limited to Brazil.—Indeed, it is widespread throughout almost all of Latin America—as well as Italy, Greece, Cyprus, Portugal, Romania, Armenia, Turkey, and most of the countries of the Arab world and Sub-Saharan Africa. Though the terminology used to describe this phenomenon differs from one place to another, the general concept of a *coronel*–client connection affects family relationships, business, politics, and many aspects of day-to-day life.

A similar term, "clientelism," is often used in many parts of the English-speaking world. However clientelism sometimes carries a negative association with corruption, which is not really related to the Brazilian concept of *coronelismo*. The term "clientelism" was popularized in the United States by the 2002 working paper of the US Agency for International Development titled "Clientelism, Patrimonialism, and Democratic Governance."[6] Although Derek Brinkerhoff and Arthur Goldsmith, who wrote this report, did not invent this term, their report helped to bring it into widespread use. Their stated goal in the report was to provide "guidance for understanding and analyzing these veiled sources of power and influence, and suggest strategies for tackling them." This stated goal describes perfectly what is meant by the Brazilian concept of *coronelismo*.

We emphasize here that *coronelismo* is not the same as cronyism, although the two can be intertwined. Cronyism is the appointment of friends and relatives to positions of authority without regard for their qualifications. Unlike *coronelismo*, cronyism has no reciprocal bonds and the recipient is not expected to perform well, if at all. Cronyism certainly does exist in Brazil. But cronyism is something separate from *coronelismo*.

It is interesting to consider the history of *coronelismo*. Although the *coronel*–client relationship dates back to the earliest days of colonial Brazil, the term *coronelismo* developed its uniquely Brazilian characteristics during the party machine politics of Brazil's Old Republic period (1889–1930). During this period, Brazil was divided into something resembling informal fiefdoms, each of which was controlled by it own recognized *coronel* (a mix of charismatic personal leader and wealthy oligarch). The term *coronel* is no longer tied to the Old Republic politics from which it derived, and the term is now widely used throughout Brazil and even abroad. For example, the British newsmagazine *The Economist* ran an obituary following the August 13, 2014, death in an airplane crash of the Brazilian presidential candidate Eduardo Campos. The article included the phrase "there was in Mr. Campos more than a trace of the old-fashioned political boss (a coronel, as they called them in the Northeast)."[7] This quotation is informative in two ways. First, it reflects the reality that since the end of the Old Republic, *coronel* does not carry much of a negative connotation. Second, it suggests that the term is more prevalent in the poorer Northeast than in the wealthier southern and southeastern states.

In talking with Brazilians, most people from the South and Southeast will deny that *coronelismo* exists at all in their regions, which may be true if we are limiting ourselves to the association with old party machine politics. Conversely, in terms of a deeply rooted system of interactions based on personal relationships, these objections are not well founded. The Brazilian concepts of *chefe, diretor, executivo, patrão, senhor, empregador*, and *patrono* all suggest the personalized and interconnected sense of a protector, advocate, and relationship builder. Those who live in southern Brazil may not accept that they have a *coronel* per se; but most Brazilians, wherever they live, would recognize that they are part of a web of intertwined and highly personalized loyalties. It is in this sense that we use the word *coronelismo* here.

Coronelismo's relationships act as a vast and complex system. Each *coronel* almost always depends on yet another *coronel* higher up. At the highest levels, the top *coronels* themselves interact with each other, forming alliances of favors given and owed as well. Although *coronel*–client systems often include family ties (nepotism), the system reaches much farther than just one's relatives. Blood relatives are generally among the *coronel*'s clients because a family relationship is assumed to guarantee loyalty. Nevertheless, in the *coronel*–client relationship, the *coronel* very often favors clients who are not related by blood. *Coronelismo* depends less on advancing one's own personal family than on those who owe loyalty. The end goal is to have the ability to smooth the way for getting things done. As a result, if a nonrelative is better able to accomplish a particular goal than a family member, the *coronel* will favor the nonrelative.

CORONELISMO AND CLIENTELISM

It bears repeating that in Brazil the concept of *coronelismo* is thought of as a good thing. For most Brazilians, *coronelismo* is condemnable only when others use it; but (and this is a big but) the same system is good in the specific interaction of the individual Brazilian with his or her own *coronel*. In this sense *coronelismo* is not quite the same thing as clientelism. As far back as 1974, Robert Kaufman laid out the principles of clientelism as being neither right nor wrong but only differently viewed across cultures.[8] Kaufman explained that though the nature of clientelism often changes markedly from one society to another, where it does exist, three features characterize the system. The relationship is

1. between people of unequal power and status;
2. self-regulating and dependent on both patron and client reciprocally playing their part (and which ends if the favor owed is not honored); and
3. based on individual ties and relationships (particularistic) and private (rather than based on governmental laws or regulation).

Again, these three features describe well what Brazilians see as *coronelismo*.

In 1999 the sociologist and Brazil expert Robert Gay was among the first to try to explain that within a Brazilian context, clientelism was not an innately negative approach to authority and leadership.[9] Gay's article, titled "Rethinking Clientelism: Demands, Discourses and Practices in Contemporary Brazil," was groundbreaking in the way that he set clientelism in a Brazilian context. In the opening paragraphs of the article, Gay writes that "clientelism is indeed an essential and enduring feature of the Brazilian political landscape." We would add that it is essential and enduring on the business and general social landscapes, as well. Gay goes on to argue (though, again, in a political science context) that, "under certain circumstances, clientelism plays a positive and largely unheralded role" (p. 7). Note again that these definitions, as related to Brazil, dissociate any negative or corrupt connotations from Brazilian clientelism, or, as we use the term, *coronelismo*.

HOW BRAZILIANS USE *CORONELISMO*

Knowing that Brazilian *coronelismo* is not associated with corruption, we also see better how it comes into play in a society in which the rule of law and governmental oversight are unreliably administered over very long periods. *Coronelismo* enables people to get things done that they would not otherwise be able to do. In a country where bribery and corruption are widespread, *coronelismo* is actually a form of protection. Because the *coronel*– client system is by its nature particularistic, the *coronel* ensures a hearing for those whose voices would otherwise not be heard. In this instance, many Brazilians view the *coronel* as their guarantor, a trusted framework against marauding elites and government bureaucrats.

All this is to say that though a *coronel* may not play a significant role in North America, where this type of personalized network is seen as biased and unfair, this is not the case in Brazil. Our challenge, then, is twofold. First, Brazilians relate to *coronelismo* but do not always relate to the actual terminology. That is to say, they do it, but they do not attach any terminology to it. Second, North Americans have a similar term, clientelism, but this word has the wrong negative connotation. Our recommendation is that you recognize that in Brazil, this *coronelismo* framework works—at least on an individual basis—and that it is thus effective and efficient. When working with Brazilians, you will experience their efforts to put you in contact with people who can open doors and remove obstacles.

We have a Brazilian friend who is our *coronel* of sorts. Délcio would never think of himself in those terms, but he is clearly one of those people who opens doors and removes obstacles. Maricá is, or was, a small fishing village just north of Rio de Janeiro and Niterói. With urban expansion, in some ways Maricá is losing its traditional look and feel. We wanted a chance to meet some of the traditional local artists and fisherman. Délcio helped us get to Maricá, made arrangements for us to stay at a local inn, introduced us to the local political leaders, and took us to meet some of the old artists: basket weavers, tapestry designers, and fishermen. Photo 5.2 shows an old canoe that belonged to a seventy-year-old fisherman. He still goes out every evening to fish from the old hollowed-out log. In investigating how old the canoe was, all the old fisherman could tell us was that his father before him always had that canoe. This photo represents for us the best of *coronelismo* because alone we would never have been able to connect with the local artists and fisherman. For Délcio it was a pleasure to use his connections to help us, and for us there is sense of gratitude and loyalty to him that will exist forever.

EXAMPLES OF BRAZILIAN AUTHORITY

Because the government provides extensive services, there is much evidence of the role that government plays in the daily life of its citizens. Photo 5.3 shows the office of Serviço de Atendimento ao Cidadão (SAC; Citizen Service Center) in Salvador, Bahia. What is impressive about this service is its location, within the local shopping mall. Inside this government center,

5.2 Meet the Local Fisherman
Canoes of the local fisherman, whom we met through our *coronel*.

customers can fill out identification cards, voter registration forms, health certificates, and applications for retirement benefits; pay bills; check up on regional services; and take care of many other government services. Note that the sign in the photograph specifically claims to handle more than eight hundred government services. The fact that this service is offered as a one-stop location inside a shopping mall is extremely innovative, and something that is unique to Brazil.

The second photograph, 5.4, also comes from the same SAC office. In the poster, citizens are reminded that they need to keep their identification documents current. The girl shown has let so much time elapse without renewing her documents, the photo suggests, that her hair has grown long enough to spill beyond her identification card. The photo humorously reminds us, *Não deixe seu documento esperar por mais tempo. Retire-o aqui* (Don't allow your document to wait any longer. Renew it here). The use of humor is an effective way to help remind people of their duty to keep their documents current, but not come across as pushy or aggressive. And finally, the fact that this advertising poster

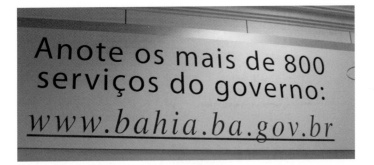

5.3 Citizen Service Center
Citizen Service Center inside
a shopping mall.

5.4 Time for a New Identification Card
Time for this girl to renew her
identification card.

is located outside the SAC office in the shopping mall all come together in this photo.

Photo 5.5 illustrates how those in positions of authority take on the responsibility to inform and teach citizens. Similar to warnings about the health risks of smoking that tobacco products in the United States carry, Brazilian tobacco products also carry a warning. The difference is that Brazilian tobacco products have extremely graphic illustrations. The graphic picture on Brazilian products is accompanied by the caption *O Ministério da Saúde adverte: Este produto contém substâncias tóxicas que*

5.5 Graphic Health Warnings
This product contains toxic substances that cause illness and death.

levam ao adoecimento e à morte. Pare de fumar. Disque saúde 136 (The Ministry of Health warns: This product contains toxic substances that cause illness and death. Stop smoking. Call health 136). There are dozens of different illustrations that accompany tobacco products in Brazil, and each has a shockingly graphic representation that is simply not found in the United States.

Similarly, we remember recently walking in Tenente Siqueira Campos Park, located on Avenida Paulista in São Paulo. In the park there are garbage bins that have different holes for recyclable waste—one hole for paper, plastic, and metal; and another hole for glass products. The bins are covered with illustrations that depict lovers, both gay and straight, in various positions, poses, and embraces. To those without knowledge of this part of town, these seem to be odd illustrations for a garbage can! But it is helpful to know that there is always a large number of couples who go to this park to make out. The illustrations are part of a campaign to promote safe sex, but they also provide an interesting example of how social agencies try to teach citizens.

Because the government and the military have always had a strong presence in Brazil, law enforcement branches have a strong visible presence as well. Especially in recent years, the

5.6 Brazilian Law Enforcement
Police presence to maintain control at sporting events.

government has tried to reassert itself in locations that have experienced a lot of violence. Foreigners will not be accustomed to the long list of different branches of law enforcement—the Federal Police, Military Police, Civil Police, Metropolitan Civil Guards, and many more. There is a delicate balance between law enforcement and the public at large. On one hand, Brazilians are leery of the police, their brutality, and their dishonesty. On the other hand, they appreciate police attempts to control Brazil's violence. Photo 5.6 was taken at a sporting event in Salvador, Bahia. In it you can see that various branches of the police force were present near the stadium.

Most people who have gone to Brazil will attest to the importance of gatekeepers—literally, folks who monitor the entrance to a building. It may be the security guard at a store, the doorman at an apartment, or the uniformed staff in front of the elevator at the entrance of businesses. Brazil has many gatekeepers, and they exemplify another area of authority. Especially in larger cities, most people live in apartment complexes. These complexes are generally surrounded by gated walls, and access into them

5.7 Apartment Doorman
Friend or foe? Apartment gatekeepers will always know.

begins with the gatekeepers who open the outside doors, open the garages for the cars, and who control all information that is passed on to the residents. It is wise to show respect for the authority of the gatekeeper and to stay on his or her good side. If you happen to come to live in the apartment complex, they will become your best helper. If you are visiting another person, they become your only access into the building. Gatekeepers are vested with authority. They facilitate or prohibit interactions. Photo 5.7 is of one of our apartment doorman, Antonio.

Another form of authority in Brazil is demonstrated by the relationship that people have with their domestic worker or maid. Historically, almost every family has had a maid in Brazil. In fact, it is not uncommon for a maid to have a maid. In some ways, that maid becomes integrated into the family. Maids become part of the family discussions, they sit and watch the nightly soap operas with the family, and they play an important part in raising and taking care of children. In recent years Brazil has initiated new laws to ensure the fair treatment of maids. The new Lei das empregadas domésticas (Domestic Maids' Law) stipulates that maids must be given regular hours, time for breaks, payment for overtime, vacations, social security benefits, and the like. Those

5.8 The Maid
Dona Rose preparing exquisite Bahian cuisine.

that hire maids are now required to declare the payment on their taxes. It is a very interesting change, simply because the presence of a maid has been such a traditional characteristic of Brazilian society. For some people, a maid simply represents the hiring of a person to help out with tasks. However, for others, the presence of a maid is seen as a continuation of the master–slave dynamic of the old *casa grande e senzala* (big house and slave quarters). What is clear is that the new laws are going to change the way families hire and interact with maids. For most part, the maid is more than just a hired worker; she is also a member of the family, as in photo 5.8 of our dear Dona Rose.

HOW TO USE WHAT YOU KNOW ABOUT AUTHORITY TO ENCOURAGE GOOD COMMUNICATION

Issues of power and authority can be difficult to discuss and interpret. As we have seen for Brazil, it is important to have some historical context and to understand how the dynamic has developed over time. Keep this in mind as you follow our recommendations on how to succeed in your interactions with Brazilians.

Dar um jeito

It is difficult to overstate how much Brazilians identify with the phrase *dar um jeito*—or, as they say, *jeitinho* (a tiny *jeito*). Brazilians will figure out a way to get around a rule, sidestep a procedure, find a friend to ease a situation, or talk with someone who has influence. Often, in North American culture, we are raised to trust in the system. In the United States there is a general sense that laws work in our favor and rules exist to make things fair for everyone. This, however, is not the attitude of Brazilians. Their starting point is more often one where rules and laws are unfairly complex, difficult, or unnecessary, and that they exist to favor the wealthy and privileged. Thus, it only makes sense that people figure out how to get around them. It is an important issue for foreigners to understand because it becomes an ethical dilemma of sorts for those who are not used to the system. If one is used to trusting the system, it can feel wrong to use various means to go around it. We are not, of course, referring to clearly immoral actions like taking a bribe; but in everyday situations, you need a little *jeito*.

A great example of this comes from an American student who was recently in Brazil, staying with a Brazilian host family. One day the American student needed some information, which could be obtained by the Brazilian host family's bank. As they walked into the bank (at closing time), there was an extremely long line of other customers who were already waiting to be taken care of. The host mother walked past all the others in line and went directly to a friend of hers who was an employee at the bank. In a few minutes their information was secured and they went home. The American student did not know how to react. On one hand, she was relieved to have gotten the needed information and documents. But on the other hand, she felt a little uncomfortable about the way that they passed in front of the others in line at the bank. From the perspective of the Brazilian host family, however, this was a simple issue of talking directly with someone who could help resolve the problem. In everyday situations, you need a little *jeito*.

Our recommendation is that you follow the Brazilian lead in getting things done. Brazilians go out of their way to be obliging.

They understand that bureaucracy is complex, and they are going to want to help you out. Let them do so. They will make phone calls on your behalf and will introduce you to others who might be able to help, and they will accompany you on visits. The truth is that sometimes you will feel that all the *jeito* takes time and effort; but remember that Brazilians offer their *jeito* out of a desire to help.

Use Names and Titles to Show Respect

It is easy, when confronted with a frustrating maze of rules and laws, to forget the basics—being respectful. Brazilian culture is informal in many ways, but it is also a culture that shows respect for others, particularly in how people address one another. One way that Brazilians show respect is in the titles they give to others. Unlike many other countries, Brazilians use people's first names, even in formal situations, but they are certain to include appropriate titles. Do not be surprised to hear a doctor referred to as Doutor Marcos or a professor called Professor Daniel. The use of first names allows for the informality that Brazilians like, but the use of the title allows for the respect that is due as well. Even at school and at work, if there is a list of people, it will be alphabetized by their first names.

Out of respect, titles are also given to people who do not have an official position. That is to say, once a person gets a little older, there is a chance that others will begin to use a title with their names. For example, when the man at the corner store named João gets to be fifty years old or so, others may call him Seu João, which means something like "Mr. John." When a woman reaches the same age, she may take on the title *dona*, as in Dona Maria.

Another way to show respect in Portuguese is to use honorific pronouns. That is to say, the word for "you" in Portuguese is *você*. However, to show more respect, Brazilians will use *o senhor* or *a senhora* instead of *você*: *A senhora quer comer?* instead of *Você quer comer?* (Do you want to eat?). When speaking with bosses, government officials, or people with whom we deal professionally, it is also common to use *o senhor* or *a senhora*. In fact, even children who would normally use *você* with their parents can be heard using the honorific form with a hint of sarcasm—"*Não senhora!*"

Although we say that Brazilians use first names, they are also very flexible in choosing whatever name happens to stick. If a person has a last name that is very distinctive, there is also a good chance that people will use that name instead. We know of a friend whose last name is Tabajara. Because it is not a common last name, everyone simply calls him Tabajara. Our guess is that almost nobody even knows that his first name is Benedito.

In the same way, if at work or school there are three people with the same first name, chances are that people will start calling somebody by a last name or a nickname. Nicknames, in fact, are very common in Brazil, and not just for little children. The use of a Brazilian's nickname, we should point out, is less a sign of closeness than it might be in North America or, for that matter, anywhere else in Latin America. Nicknames act as an identifier more than a sign of familiarity. It is not uncommon for Brazilians to know only the nickname of some people with whom they would consider themselves on good terms. This is even more the case for famous people. For example, all Brazilians and most of the rest of the soccer-playing world know the Brazilian national hero Pelé, even if that same worldwide audience might not know his given name, Edison Arantes do Nascimento. Perhaps the best example of how using nicknames is respectful in Brazil is the case of Lula. Brazil's former president, Luiz Inácio da Silva, was universally known as "Lula," a name he used even in formal settings. In fact, in 1982, he actually officially added "Lula" to his name.

Brazilians are also likely to look at a person's physical characteristics and give them a nickname that relates. If you are extremely tall or have a big nose or bright red hair, look out, because chances are that you will get a nickname to match. For example, one of Brazil's most famous colonial-age sculptors was a man named Antônio Francisco Lisboa, who is better known as Aleijadinho (the Little Cripple), because of his disfigured body, probably a result of leprosy. Portuguese language speakers make extensive use of the diminutive forms *inho* and *inha* and the augmentive forms *ão* and *ã*. Consequently, it is common to add these endings on to people's names, as a term of endearment: Marquinho, Joãozinho, Martinha, Clarinha, Filipão, Orlandão.

The Takeaway

When you deal with Brazilians, ask them what name they prefer to be called. Do not assume that it is more polite to use a person's last name. There are many who simply use a first name or a nickname, even in professional situations. Once you ask and know his or her preference, you can use the name without feeling that you are showing a lack of respect or formality. If a person does have a title, it is nice to use that title, and we recommend that you use it without worrying about sounding too formal or stuffy. As to the use of *o senhor* or *a senhora*, although it is true that Brazilians use the honorific forms, foreigners who have limited Portuguese language skills can safely use *você*. If, however, your Portuguese language skills get better, then you will naturally catch on to when it is important to use *o senhor* or *a senhora*. And you will catch on through observation.

FOLLOW THE RULES AND PROCEDURES

Foreigners find that Brazilian companies and government agencies often have rules that they may feel are excessive or unnecessary. For example, it may be that upon entering the offices or factory of a company they will ask you to bring a passport, provide them with an identification card, and take a photograph of you as you enter. Although such things happen at various companies all over the world, in Brazil it seems to happen more often then one would expect and in locations that do not make sense.

Our recommendation is that you go with the flow and submit to the extra procedures. Given our discussion about *jeito*, if there is a way to minimize all the procedural requests, then chances are that your Brazilian contacts will do what they can. Until then, you should expect to confront unusual rules or procedures more than you normally do.

The LESCANT category of authority is important because it teaches us to look at how power is culturally based. Brazil is a country where there is a larger gap between those who have power and those who do not. Many rules and laws have been set up, for a variety of different reasons, and they can be confusing or frustrating to foreigners. Brazilians have found different ways to cope with these rules and laws, and we have much to learn from them. When we understand these issues, we will start to relate to the Brazilian senses of *dar um jeito, malandro,* and *coronelismo.*

SUMMARY OF THE BRAZILIAN AUTHORITY CONCEPTION

What we know about Brazil's views on authority:

Brazilian government and politics
- Colonial beginnings relied on exports to those in power—sugarcane, coffee, gold, precious stones, and raw materials.
- Modern shift to balance an export-driven economy with a desire to develop nationalist populist interests.
- Fernando Henrique's Plano Real exemplified the export globalist approach, and the Lula/Dilma presidencies, with programs like Bolsa Familia and Fome Zero, help to appease populist interests.

Brazil views of outside authority
- Brazil has grown tired of being exploited by outsiders.
- Foreign investors should show that they are committed to Brazil for the long term.
- As a result, it takes 108 days to start a business in Brazil, with many cumbersome, heavy, and taxing laws.

Authority and corruption
- Estimates are that the annual cost of corruption in Brazil is between 1.38 and 2.3 percent of the country's total GDP.
- There have been increased public demonstrations in response to misuse of authority (e.g., Vem pra rua).

Malandro
- *Malandro* is a person who is street-smart, clever, a finagler, a manipulator—one who can work around the system to get things done.

Coronelismo
- Leadership style where a person of influence bestows favors to remove obstacles in getting things done.

- Although many Brazilians will not recognize this practice by name, few deny it in principle—that is, a web of intertwined and personalized loyalties.

Communication strategies on how to deal with Brazil's views on authority:

Recommendations
- *Dar um jeito or dar um jeitinho*
  - A phrase that implies an ability to get around a rule, sidestep a procedure, or talk with someone who has influence.
  - Recognize that Brazilian bureaucracy is complex and they are going to want to work around the system.
  - Do not think of *jeitinho* as something underhanded; it is simply a sense of how to work around things to get things done.
- Showing respect in speech
  - Do not confuse Brazilian informality with a lack of respect.
  - Use titles with those who have academic degrees or positions of power.
- Following rules and procedures
  - Go with the flow of the extra rules and procedures that Brazilian companies require.
- Allow your Brazilian friends to use their *jeitinho.*

6

BRAZILIAN
Nonverbal
Communication

One Kiss Or Two?

Nonverbal communication covers an extremely large number of topics. At times it refers to the gestures that we make, how we move our body, or what we do with our eyes. At other times nonverbal communication refers to how we dress or even the colors that we wear. Nonverbal communication can also include the way people touch, how close to each other they stand or sit, or even how they respond to the way that things smell. One difficulty with nonverbal communication is that much of it goes on unconsciously. As a result, not only do we fail to recognize that our nonverbal communication is culturally based, we do not even know that we are doing it or perceiving it. As such, our challenge is to become aware of our own nonverbal communication, and then be able to compare that with those norms from other cultures.

In the case of Brazilians, there are many differences between the way that they communicate nonverbally and the way that many non-Brazilians do. In this chapter we look at a number of examples, and compare them, mainly to the norms in North American culture. We begin with body movements, called kinesics, and then discuss dress and adornment. We then deal with physical touch, called haptics; and with interpersonal distance, called proxemics. Finally, we look at passive nonverbal communication—such as how to respond to colors, symbols, or smells—and how we count.

KINESICS

Kinesics refers to the way that a person moves his or her body—their gestures, posture, and how they move their head, shoulders, hands, arms, and legs. We use the word *emblem* for nonverbal messages that translate directly into words. For example, in the United States, the "OK" gesture (a circle with the thumb and index finger and three fingers extended) is an emblem that has a direct verbal counterpart (i.e., "OK"). Many of the emblems used in Brazil either do not exist in North America or exist but mean something else. For example, as we discuss below, the "OK" sign means something very different in Brazil. What follows is a list of the most common emblems in Brazil that differ from those in the United States or Canada.

The "Thumbs-Up"/Cool Gesture

Brazilians use the "thumbs-up" sign a lot. It is the generic "OK" sign of the Brazilian. However, "thumbs-up" goes even farther in Brazil. Thumbs up can also be used to say thank you, to ask for permission, or to indicate that you are going to do something. Recently, we observed an elderly lady, probably more than seventy years old, who did a thumbs-up as she crossed the street in front of traffic in Salvador. There was something wonderfully delightful in seeing how she stopped traffic with her thumbs-up. It was as if she were saying "Hold up world, and thank you very much because, slow as I may be, I am moving through." We can guarantee that Brazilians will use a thumbs-up sign when crossing the street. We can also assure that this will be the most common emblem that visitors will observe from Brazilians. The thumbs-up gesture is sometimes accompanied by the word *legal* (legal) or *joia* (jewel), to say that something is "cool" in Portuguese.

The "OK" Gesture
The "OK" gesture, as we just noted, has an entirely different meaning in Brazil than it does in the United States or Canada. Even when they do recognize the OK sign from North American movies and the like, Brazilians actively avoid using it. This is because there is a vulgar gesture, similar to "giving someone the finger," that looks a lot like the inverted OK sign. We recommend using the thumbs-up gesture instead; it will work better while in Brazil.

The "Come Here" Gesture
In North America there is a gesture that is made when someone says "come here." With the palm up, use your index finger to point at the person and then move the hand and index finger back toward you. It is the same gesture that is made when people say, "here kitty, kitty." Brazilians have a different gesture that is used when they say *vem cá* (come here). With the palm down, they wave jointly all four fingers in a downward motion. (By the way, the Brazilian version of "here kitty, kitty" includes the repetition of the meow sound—*miau, miau, miau*.)

Finger Snapping, Type One
In North America, people generally snap their fingers in only one way: by pressing the middle finger with the thumb until the thumb slips. Brazilians snap their fingers in two different ways. The first of these is the exact same gesture as in the United States or Canada—however, with a different interpretation of what this means.

In North America snapping fingers means "I have an idea"/"I've got it" or "I am trying to remember something." Brazilians use the same gesture of snapping fingers, but for them it means "I've been waiting for a really long time!" Usually, you will notice that they snap their fingers multiple times while also rotating their whole hand in a circle. In North America people generally only snap their fingers once, because snapping multiple times would indicate an impolite way to get someone else's attention. In Brazil, snapping multiple times is simply part of the gesture to indicate a long wait.

Finger Snapping, Type Two

Brazilians have a second type of snapping that does not exist in the United States or Canada. This is the Brazilian "hurry up" snap. This hurry up snap and sound are made by hitting the index finger into the space between the joined thumb and middle finger. It is actually a difficult maneuver to learn because it requires a rapid movement of the whole wrist, while keeping the index finger flexible. The gesture is made with the sense of hurry up, but it can also convey the meaning of "Oh no! Now what?"

The "Whatever" Gesture

The expression "whatever" has entered common usage in North America and carries the same meaning in Brazil. The Brazilian phrase for "whatever" is *tanto faz*. Frequently, this phrase is accompanied by a gesture where both hands are held vertically, with open palms toward the body and the back of the hand facing toward the person being spoken to, and then alternately sliding the fingers over each other, alternating front and back. No counterpart exists in North America, but you will see it fairly often in Brazil.

The Gesture for Cheating or Stealing

Brazilians make a gesture that implies cheating or stealing by extending the thumb, palm down, and then rolling all the fingers in a downward motion. Sometimes this thumb is held in the middle of the palm of the other hand. In North America this is limited to a handful of ethnic groups; in Brazil, everyone uses it.

The Earlobe Tug Gesture

In Brazil one way of saying that something is delicious is to pull on your earlobe. Brazilians do this by grabbing their earlobe between the thumb and index finger and gently tugging on it two or three times. In North America, this gesture is not an actual emblem. In other words, North Americans—unlike Brazilians—do not tug on their earlobe to mean something specific. Nevertheless, the earlobe tug *does* exist in North America. It acts as a subconscious adaptor (sometimes called a "tell," or nonverbal leakage), and it has an entirely different meaning than in Brazil.

As the forensic psychologist Lydia Pozzato explains, tugging the ear shows discomfort.[1] Pozzato goes on to suggest that in a North American setting, this is a blocking gesture related to the way that children cover their ears when they do not want to hear something or are being overwhelmed: "These instinctive reactions stay with people throughout their lives. Only as they mature, and learn how to disguise their discomfort more subtly, does one see the hands-over-the-ears movement reduced to a subtle tug on the ear lobe." So a Canadian in Brazil might well interpret an overt Brazilian nonverbal gesture of something positive as a subtle North American gesture of discomfort or hiding something—and that is quite a difference in interpretation!

The "Hooking-Up" Gesture
To indicate that two people are hanging out together, dating, and getting into a relationship, Brazilians hold both hands out, palms down, fists closed with the index fingers extended. Next, they rub the two index fingers together back and forth. This gesture has no meaning at all in a North American context.

The "Who Knows?" Chin Rub Gesture
In North American culture, people shrug their shoulders as an emblem gesture that means "who knows?" Brazilians also do the exact same shoulder shrug, with the exact same meaning. However, Brazilians have another entirely different gesture that means "who knows?" This gesture, totally unknown in North America, is made by rubbing the back of your fingers in one outward motion against the bottom of your chin. Many times this gesture is made while saying the phrase *sei lá*, which also means "who knows?"

The "I'm the Best" Chin Pat Gesture
The gesture, which means "I'm the best" or "Look at me!" is similar to the chin-rubbing gesture for "who knows?" Brazilians

make this gesture by patting the bottom of their chin with their fingers. This is a subtly different form of the "who knows?" gesture. When Brazilians *pat* their chin (as opposed to rubbing it), the meaning changes.

The "Talk to You Later" Gesture
You may see a Brazilian point to her mouth with one hand and then close her fist and move her hands in front of her, open up the index fingers of both hands, and twirl them around each other. If so, she is telling you that she will talk to you later.

The Phone Gesture
When Brazilians use a gesture to ask someone to call them on the phone, chances are they will hold their closed hand up to their ear, extending their thumb and little finger to make the shape of a receiver. Although this gesture is also used to some extent in the United States and Canada, it is far more common in Brazil. Brazilians often accompany the phone gesture with the phrase *te ligo* (I'll call you) or *me liga* (call me).

The "That's Expensive!" Gesture
Brazilians have a gesture to indicate that something is expensive that has no counterpart in the United States or Anglophone Canada. (It is used by some Francophone Canadians.) To make the gesture, Brazilians hold one hand up, with all the fingers touching the thumb. They then circle the fingertips of that hand in small motions around the thumb.

The Lower-Eyelid-Tug Gesture
Brazilians have an emblem gesture in which they place their index finger just under their eye, and then pull the skin down a bit. In Brazil this tug-at-the-lower-eyelid gesture means "I'm watching you!" This gesture does not mean anything in the United States, but the same gesture has a significantly different meaning in Francophone Canada (and is used as a borrowed gesture in parts of Anglophone Canada). In Francophone Canada (as well as the rest of the French-speaking world), this gesture means "I don't believe you." The phrase *mon oeil* (my eye) often accompanies it

(said in French or English, depending on the speaker's language). In Canada the meaning is much stronger than in the Brazilian version. When Brazilians use this eye-tug gesture, it is just their way of saying "be careful, I'm watching you."

The "No, No, No" Gesture
Not only do Brazilians hold up a vertical index finger and shake it to indicate "no, no, no," but they do so while also making a clicking sound, similar to the North American clicking sound that means, "tsk, tsk, tsk"; but here it means "no, no, no."

The "Meeting Is Over" Gesture
When getting together in a business context with Brazilians, it is hard to know when a meeting is really over. At some point, however, the person who is in charge will hold both hands out, close together, palms down, and with a horizontal motion back and forth alternating which hand is on the top and which is on the bottom. This indicates that the meeting is, in fact, over. Without this gesture, it is impossible to know. After this gesture is made, you will notice that everyone stands up and leaves.

The "Horn" Gesture
We have bad news for fans of the University of Texas Longhorns football and basketball teams. The "hook 'em Horns" gesture may be the symbol of your mascot, referring to longhorn cattle, but in Brazil the same emblem is a vulgar expression that refers to a man who has been cheated on by a spouse or girlfriend. Imagine how shocking it is for Brazilians to attend a Texas Longhorns football game and witness 100,000 people simultaneously making the *cornudo* gesture! Our recommendation for the Texans is to stick with the "thumbs-up" gesture as much as possible when in Brazil!

AFFECT DISPLAY: HOW, EXACTLY, ARE YOU FEELING?

In addition to emblems, other aspects of kinesics differ between cultures. One of these is called "affect display." Affect display

BRAZILIAN NONVERBAL COMMUNICATION

relates to how much or how little a person displays an emotion. Two people who are equally happy may not demonstrate that happiness in the same way. In North America we sometimes talk about "wearing your heart on your sleeve."

In very basic terms, a Brazilian displays emotions more openly than most North Americans do. This is not to say that Brazilians have stronger emotions—or are more happy, angry, disgusted, or surprised than North Americans. Rather, Brazilian society considers it more socially acceptable for people to show their emotions openly. For example, when a Brazilian's soccer team scores a goal, there is a good chance that we will see a person actually get up off the couch and dance around the room. When a North American's football team scores a touchdown, you may see a fist pump. Both may be equally happy for their team, but there are cultural norms for how much we are allowed to express those emotions.

The absence of affect displays can have a real impact on how people relate to one another. Brazilians often think of North Americans as being cold and uncaring. They are likely to feel this way even when their North American counterpart is feeling just as strongly what the Brazilian is feeling. The disconnect in such situations is simply because North Americans do not display their emotions as openly. The flip side of this is also true. North Americans often think that Brazilians are exceptionally emotional—friendly, sad, angry, or excitable. Here, too, both parties may have exactly the same intensity of feeling; but the Brazilians are simply culturally more accustomed to displaying emotions more openly than the North Americans. The important lesson here is to avoid presuming that emotions are displayed equally from one culture to another. Although exceptions exist, generally speaking Brazilians display emotions more openly than most North Americans do.

In photo 6.1, you will see our Brazilian friend, on the left, having dinner with a US friend, on the right. At the time, the two had just met. The Brazilian is very open with her hugs and physical affection. The American is generally quite reserved. In the photograph, however, it looks like they are best friends. We show this photo because recently this same American was

6.1 Best Friends
They look like best friends, but are they? Actually, they just met.

saying goodbye to a dear friend of hers, whom she would not see again for years. Despite this, their goodbye hug was minimal, even though the true emotion of saying goodbye was intense. The emotion that accompanied the event in this photograph was much less intense than the emotion of the goodbye. However, because of the Brazilian's affect display, there is a feeling (from a US perspective at least) of high emotion in the photograph.

An example of affect display from the Brazilian point of view is the reaction that Brazilians have to the way that North Americans close car doors. North Americans have a tendency, at least as perceived by Brazilians, to slam car doors. Perhaps it is because North American cars are generally larger and heavier. In Brazil a slammed car door is a signal of anger, and Brazilians misinterpret the emotion of closing car doors. When in Brazil, exert care to close car doors softly. It will make a big difference in how you are perceived.

Car honking evokes the opposite misunderstanding. North Americans perceive the honking of a horn as a sign of anger. Brazilians, however, simply honk a horn to make people aware that a car is coming by. The result is a great deal more horn-blowing in Brazil than even in the most congested traffic of Los Angeles, New York, or Vancouver. North Americans misinterpret the honking and believe that the Brazilians are angry, when in reality they are not.

OCULESICS

Related to kinesics is the concept of oculesics. Oculesics refers to the way that people use their eyes, such as eye contact, eye rolling, winking, and gazing at people. Oculesics also includes looking away and *not* looking at someone. North Americans will find that Brazilians are similar in the way that they expect a person to look at others when they are talking. That should not cause any difficulty. What is different is the amount of time that men are allowed to stare at a woman before it would be perceived as inappropriate. In North American culture, a man can take a quick peek at a woman, and there will be no sense of discomfort. However, if the man were to maintain eye contact and gaze at the woman for more than a couple of seconds, the woman would most likely begin to feel uncomfortable. In Brazil men gaze at women much longer, and they pass their eyes from head to toe.

In the United States especially, staring at a woman's body in the workplace constitutes sexual harassment, which is punishable by law. But in Brazil the exact behavior that is unlawful in the United States is not necessarily offensive. This is not to say that Brazilian men are somehow more depraved. It simply means that the United States and Brazil differ on what is appropriate and inappropriate in this regard. At this point, it is important to note that it actually *is* possible in Brazil for a man to stare too long at a woman, but the cultural norm allows for a longer look before it crosses the threshold of being inappropriate and causing discomfort. Our recommendation, especially for women, is to be aware that women do get looked at with a longer gaze and to simply ignore it.

The reverse is also true. Brazilian women differ in how they make eye contact with men, especially if they are coworkers and know each other. North American men may misinterpret the more intense eye contact from Brazilian woman as flirtatious. This is especially possible given the fact that Brazilians comment on a person's appearance more than North Americans do.

DRESS AND ADORNMENT

There are clear differences in the way that North Americans and Brazilians dress. Part of this is related to climate and region, of course. Even in the United States, professional attire in Los Angeles may look different from professional attire in Philadelphia. If we had to be honest, writing this chapter makes us nervous, because we realize that there is a fine line between stereotypes and average tendencies. This is especially the case when we are dealing with appearance. What follows are some general guidelines and suggestions related to dress and adornment in Brazil.

Brazilians have a comfort with bodies and different body shapes. Given that most of the population of Brazil lives close to the coast, there is a strong identity with the beach and beach culture. Some specific regions of the United States—Hawaii and coastal Florida, for example—share in this identity. The difference is that in Brazil, this is much more the norm. To get a sense of this, it is useful for visitors to spend time observing people at Brazilian beaches. On a visit to Copacabana and Ipanema on Sunday mornings, for example, one finds the streets are closed to automobile traffic. On these mornings it is common to see families that come together to stroll along the beach. It is not uncommon to see a grandmother in her bikini, walking or being pushed in a wheelchair, along the *calçadão* (sidewalk), hand in hand with a daughter and a granddaughter. There is something beautiful about this scene of these generations of sunbathers together—and very different from what you would expect to see in North America.

Although many Brazilians are fitness conscious, people with bodies of all shapes and sizes stroll along the beaches. Brazilians simply identify with their beaches in a personal way, and

BRAZILIAN NONVERBAL COMMUNICATION

139

6.2 Itapuã Beach
Getting into Brazilian beach culture with a serving of *acarajé*.

exposed bodies are part of this identity. Photo 6.2 also illustrates another vital part of beach life, buying food items from the vendors that pass by. In this photo we see a generous portion of *acarajé* (shrimp fritter) at Itapuã in Bahia. In terms of nonverbal communication, the level of comfort that Brazilians have about bodies stands out as a contrast to the North American norm.

In reference to body shapes, the following photo shows some of the bronze statues of the Meninas do Brasil (Brazilian Girls), also affectionately called the Gordinhas de Ondina (Ondina Fat Girls), located near the Ondina Beach in Salvador, Bahia. These were created by the Bahian plastic artist Eliana Kertéz to show the charm and beauty of real women. It shows again the comfort level that Brazilians feel for body shapes. In the photo one of the authors is standing in front of the statue of Catarina.

Clothing in Professional Settings

As a general rule of thumb, we can say that in professional settings Brazilians are image and fashion conscious. Compared

6.3 Ondina Fat Girls
Statues of the Gordinhas de Ondina (Ondina Fat Girls), to show the charm and beauty of women of all shapes and sizes.

with most North Americans, most Brazilians pay considerably more attention to the brands, the types of accessories, and the cleanliness of their clothing. Like North Americans, Brazilians are very hygiene conscious as well—but what Brazilians and North Americans emphasize in this regard differs. Brazilians bathe multiple times per day. Most North Americans bathe no more than once a day. Likewise, Brazilians brush their teeth several times a day, while most North Americans do so once in the morning and once at night (while using breath mints if needed in between). Brazilians notice, unfavorably and surprisingly, how little North Americans brush their teeth. As to the use of deodorants, North Americans and Brazilians do so at roughly the same rate (90 percent use), so this is less a matter of body odor than of perceived freshness of appearance.[2]

Perhaps a key word to describe Brazilian professional dress is "polished." Brazilian women do not wear a lot of bold-colored makeup, but they do take care to manicure their nails, take care of their skin, remove body hair, and keep a natural look. In much of the United States and Anglophone Canada, such personal hygiene issues are optional and may well represent a political position on gender roles. This is simply not the case in Brazil. A woman who does not manicure her nails, for instance, is not taking a stand but rather just someone with bad hygiene.

Likewise, Brazilian men try to have a polished look. They wear leather shoes more than sneakers, slacks more than denim, and button-down shirts more than T-shirts and polo shirts. Greater care is given to hair care among men than in the United States or Canada as well. It is, for instance, much more common to see men combing their hair in a public restroom in Brazil.

The type of Brazilian professional attire a person wears also relates to the position of the person. It is common to see uniforms, dresses, shirts, coats, and ties for those who have service-oriented jobs or for those in lower-management positions. However, those in upper-management positions dress in more of a business casual style. For men there is almost no need to dress in a coat and tie when doing business with Brazilians. The exception to this is perhaps when meeting with financial institutions in São Paulo.

Men's Professional Dress

For men, polished leather shoes, pressed slacks, and a button-down, long-sleeved shirt are generally accepted. Given Brazilians' attention to detail, let us look at these pieces in a little more detail.

Polished Shoes

Brazil is one of the centers of the footwear industry, ranking third in the world, and people notice shoes. First, this means that you should be wearing shoes that *can be* polished—usually leather shoes and not running shoes. Second, Brazilians polish their shoes regularly and notice when North American and Canadian visitors do not do so. They also notice when shoes are scuffed or worn down at the heels.

Pressed Slacks

Most Brazilians pay considerably more attention to whether their clothing is wrinkled than do the majority of their North

American counterparts. They will notice when slacks (and shirts) are freshly laundered and pressed. You will notice that in Brazil, many people have domestic maids to do this laundry work. If not, they send their clothes out to be professionally laundered.

Button-Down, Long-Sleeved Shirts

In both the United States and Canada, two main business dress codes exist for men. The first is business formal, which includes the traditional suit, tie, and long-sleeved, button-down shirt. Although this does appear in some sectors in Brazil (e.g., the finance and banking sector in São Paulo), it is far less widespread than it is in the United States or Canada. The second North American business dress option is business casual. What passes for business casual in North America, however, never caught on in Brazil. To a Brazilian, the absence of a jacket and tie is business casual; what North Americans wear is just casual (not business).

Let us give a bit of background on the North American business casual dress code. In the late 1980s Steve Jobs of Apple transformed corporate dress by starting a trend of wearing a fine-quality, single-colored T-shirt under a jacket. This trend spread from the high-technology companies of Silicon Valley to many other industries and regions across the continent. By the beginning of this century, the generally accepted business dress code had morphed into what has come to be called business casual: dress pants with short-sleeved golf shirts, either with or without a jacket—and if a jacket is worn, it is possible to use designer jeans in some settings. This may be perfectly all right as business dress in the United States or Canada, but it is uncommon at best in Brazil.

Women's Professional Dress

Women in Brazil wear both dresses and pants in professional settings, but again sophistication usually trumps casualness. Shoes with heels are more popular than flat shoes. As with men's shoes, women's shoes are kept free of nicks and scuffs. All of this varies from region to region and from summer to winter. In the southern part of Brazil, the winters can be quite cold; and in the northern parts of Brazil, the days can be hot and humid. In the south people wear multiple layers when it is cold, and in the north people wear light fabrics. In broad terms, as related to style of dress, São Paulo is more like New York, whereas Rio de Janeiro is more like Miami. The Northeast of Brazil is more, perhaps, like New Orleans.

Women's styles are more difficult to describe, which is probably true everywhere. Women's professional clothing in Brazil is worn a bit tighter and tends to be more revealing than is the norm in North America. As with the men, being polished generally wins out over being casual.

Even casual clothing comes with a bit of a statement and is seldom sloppy. Hair is often worn loose, and large earrings are much more commonly worn than in the United States or Canada. In North America lipstick is optional, though it is commonly worn. In Brazil lipstick, when worn, is in softer colors. Although roughly 65 percent of US women wear foundation makeup, facial makeup in Brazil is minimal. Many Brazilian women wear jewelry, frequently semiprecious stones and gold chains. We might add that in Brazil, there are two words that are translated as jewelry: *joias* and *bijuteria*. *Joias* are the fine pieces of jewelry made from gold and gemstones. *Bijuteria* are the less expensive trinkets and ornaments. Brazilian jewelry, both *joias* and *bijuteria*, can be extremely creative, with everything from Brazilian semiprecious stones to those made from the seeds of indigenous plants. And women wear quite a bit of both types.

Attire in Casual Settings

In casual settings Brazilian attire depends a lot on location. When going out for the evening, people in Brazil like to dress up, but casual shorts and T-shirts are also acceptable. For running around town, flip-flops are worn in many instances where North Americans would wear sneakers. When exercising, women especially wear more tight-fitting tops. You will never see a Brazilian woman in shorts and a baggy T-shirt at the gym. When going to the beach, Brazilians are minimalists. For men this means a swimming suit, flip-flops, and a couple of dollars. For women it means a two-piece swimming suit, a sarong or light wrap, and flip-flops. Brazilians often joke about how much foreigners take to the beach. At public schools students often have school uniforms, which usually include a polo-style shirt. At universities students dress casually, in jeans, T-shirts, and tennis shoes. The teachers often dress the same.

HAPTICS AND PROXEMICS

Haptics refers to the way that people communicate through touch. In the case of haptics, there is a certain level of touch that signals a professional relationship and a different type of touch that signals a social, friendly, or even intimate relationship. Miscommunication can occur if there is a varying level of touch signals—for example, touching that means friendship to a North American, but a polite relationship to a Brazilian—and then there will be misinterpretations of the meaning behind the touch.

This, in fact, is exactly what happens between North Americans and Brazilians. A Brazilian is more apt to touch a person's arm when speaking with him or her. Brazilians also regularly lay their hand on another person's shoulder. In Brazil when people are talking, they touch each other more frequently than is common or even comfortable in the United States or Anglophone Canada. All this touching seems to enter what North Americans would interpret as friendship and warmth—or *mis*interpret as flirtation or something inappropriate. For the Brazilian, however, this touching remains in the range of nothing more than social politeness. Looking at this from the other perspective, if in a social situation an American were to touch a Brazilian in a way that felt more professional, the result would be that the American would seem rather cold or unemotional.

Because we are talking about *business* communication, it is necessary to raise the issue not only of cultural norms but also of sexual harassment. Although the definition of sexual harassment varies to some extent by state in the United States and by province in Canada, all these sexual harassment codes include the prohibition of unwelcome touching in the workplace. By most standards throughout the United States and Canada, customary Brazilian haptics can be interpreted as "unwelcome touching." In other words, what is customary and innocent touching behavior in Brazil can result in sexual harassment suits in the United States and Canada. Though we can argue that such lawsuits are groundless and reflect a lack of cultural flexibility from a Brazilian perspective, we *cannot* make the same argument if the touching behavior is taking place in the United States or Canada. And though it is hoped that cultural sensitivity would come into play if the touching were done innocently, Brazilians doing business in either country must not assume that this will be the case. As a result, there are two points here. First, North Americans should attempt to adapt to the differences in touching behavior when they go to Brazil. Second, they must forewarn Brazilians of the possibility of accusations of unwanted touching when they visit Canada or the United States.

Different Greetings

When Brazilians greet each other in professional situations, two men will simply shake hands. Brazilians' handshakes are not particularly strong, and they do not pump their arms up and down very many times. Whereas people from Canada and the northern United States pump their arms two or three times per shake and people from parts of Texas and the southern United States may shake four or five times, most Brazilians pump only two times. The grip strength varies in North America between men and women. In North America, men generally shake more firmly with each other than they do with women or than women do among themselves. By contrast, in Brazil, the grip strength does not vary between genders. The softer grip associated with shaking hands with women in North America is the standard grip for both genders in Brazil. If the two men already know each other well, they may also rest or pat their left hands on the shoulder of the other while shaking hands. If a man greets a woman in a professional situation, again, often a handshake is all that is given. If the two people already know each other, the man may give her a kiss on the cheek as well, but in professional situations this is less common. When women greet each other

6.4 One Kiss or Two?
When greeting others in casual situations, a kiss on the cheek is fine.

in professional settings, they either just extend a handshake or give a handshake and a kiss on the cheek.

Kisses on the cheek are common in Brazil, but do vary. Depending on the region, sometimes women are given two kisses, one on each cheek. In São Paulo one kiss is more common, but in most places two kisses are the norm. When people kiss on the cheek, what really happens is that people touch cheeks and kind of kiss the air. When kissing cheeks, move your head to the left, in order to kiss the woman's right cheek first. When saying goodbye, this same basic process is repeated.

In social and casual situations, men sometimes shake hands again, but generally they give each other a pat on the shoulder or a brief hug. In the case of a man and a woman or two women, a kiss on the cheek is appropriate; a handshake seems out of place. Among women, a kiss on the cheek is normal. And again, when leaving the process, this would be the same.

The major difference between North American and Brazilian patterns happens when the group is larger. When saying goodbye in the United States, for example, chances are that North Americans will shout out a general "bye everybody" to everyone. In Brazil people are more likely to give a kiss on the cheek to every woman in the room, and a brief pat on the back or shoulder to every man in the room.

Proxemics: Personal Space

Proxemics refers to the way that people use the space around them. One of the manifestations is how near or far people stand from each other when talking. Generally, it is said that North Americans like to be about an arm's length apart from others in casual conversations. In reality, the distance is determined by the arm length of the tallest person in the conversation and differs between conversations of people of the opposite sex. In North America the distance between two men is usually about the distance between the taller man's extended arm and the other man's ear. This is the same for women with women. When men and women are in conversation, however, this distance is too close. The man should be able to reach out and just miss touching the woman's nose. Any closer than this would be getting into the other person's intimate or personal space.

In Brazil people also differentiate between how far apart people of the same sex should stand in conversation versus how far apart people of the opposite sex should stand. In Brazil this distance also shifts as we go from the South (farther) to the North (closer). In the South and Southeast of Brazil, people of the *opposite* sex stand about as close together as people of the *same* sex stand in North America. In other words, the space between a man and a woman in this part of Brazil will usually be about the distance between the man's extended arm and the woman's ear. This distance between a man and woman, however, enters into intimate space for the North Americans, and men or women alike will feel uncomfortable at best and may misinterpret this distance as something sexual in nature at worst. It is good to pause and note that this closeness is definitely not sexual; it is a difference in social norm.

The distance between men or between women has no equivalent in North America—even in the southern part of Brazil, where the proxemic distance is at its farthest in the country. In this region, the space between men is smaller. It is roughly equivalent to the distance between the elbow of the taller man's extended arm and the other man's ear—or half an arm's length. The same is true of the distance between two women in a conversation.

The North American who encounters this closer stance will—quite naturally—back up a bit. The Brazilian will then move in closer again until the North American is backed up against a table or wall. Sometimes, the North American will turn slightly, to form a "V" of open space with the Brazilian. In this case, the Brazilian will naturally move back in front of the North American, creating a sort of tightly circled dance of sorts. To the North American, the Brazilian seems pushy and might literally claim that the Brazilian is "in my face." To the Brazilian, the North American seems quite literally distant and standoffish.

These distances get even shorter the farther north one goes in Brazil. People in Rio de Janeiro, for instance, stand a bit closer than people in São Paulo, but only slightly so, and this is hardly noticeable. People in Recife or Belém, in turn, stand a bit closer than people in Rio. Although this is only slightly closer than people in Rio, it is perhaps an inch or so closer than would be comfortable in São Paulo. For a North American, this is even more noticeable than it might be for Brazilians themselves.

Touching during the Conversation

Not only is it true that Brazilians tend to be closer together than North Americans when they talk together, but there is more physical touching while they are talking. They are more apt to put their hand on the other person's arm, rest their hand on the other person's shoulder, or put their whole arm around the other's shoulder. Proxemics are also different in public settings. Some North Americans are surprised when Brazilian personal space becomes nonexistent on public transportation. When the subways and buses are full, there will be zero space between people.

Brazilians also have a more open sense of public displays of affection. Couples openly hug and kiss in public, on buses, in the subway, in parks, and almost anywhere else. Photo 6.5 was taken at the Barra Lighthouse in Salvador. The fact that the couple in the photo is kissing is not surprising. What was

6.5 A Public Display of Affection
A Brazilian couple publicly display their affection, oblivious to others who might be around them.

surprising was to see the busload of Americans who arrived to see the lighthouse and then walked passed the kissing couple, not even a yard away. It did not phase the couple to have all these people walking past them, but it certainly caught the attention of the Americans.

PASSIVE NONVERBAL COMMUNICATION

In addition to the nonverbal parameters that we have discussed so far in this chapter, there are other nonverbal cues that are called passive, because they deal more with the environment around us or with things that are not related to our bodies specifically. Following are a few photographs that illustrate some of these passive nonverbal communication features.

The first photo (6.6) was taken in the elevator of an apartment building. In Brazil the ground floor is often represented with a "P," which stands for *planta* or *planta baixa*. But the ground floor is not considered to be the first floor. Notice in this photograph that the "P" floor is under the mezzanine floor,

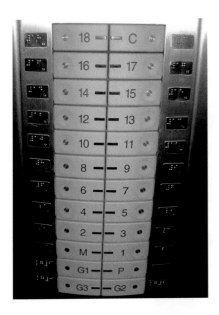

6.6 Brazilian Elevators
"P" is the ground floor, followed by "M," for mezzanine,
and then the first floor is
above that.

"M," which is then followed by the first floor, "1." This apartment
building also happens to have three underground floors for parking garages, *garagem*—G1, G2, and G2. Finally, the top floor of
this apartment has a floor on the roof with a swimming pool and
an exercise room, and this floor is designated "C," for *cobertura*.
This organization and terminology is not uncommon. The best
thing is to remember that the first floor is not the ground floor.

Handwriting changes drastically from one culture to another.
It is sometimes difficult to read handwriting because certain
letters are drawn with slight modifications. Photo 6.7 shows a
handwritten note that a maid wrote to us, requesting that we buy
a few cleaning items at the store. Notice, for example, that the
date is May 25, 2009, and the apartment number is 604. The
problem is that it is possible to misunderstand the numbers and
think that the date was March 23 and that the apartment number was 609 or 607. The 5 could be read as a 3, and the 4 looks
like a 7 or a 9. Here is what the handwritten note really says in
Portuguese, *Sr. Orlando 25/5/09 604 Gentileza providenciar os
materiais para limpeza: Agua sanitária, sapólio limão, limpa vidro,
veja limpeza pesado, veja.*

6.7 Brazilian Handwriting
Handwriting that changes
from one culture to another.

6.8 Habib's Fast Food
Habib's cartoon mascot that
would seem inappropriate
within a North American
context.

Habib's is a Brazilian fast food chain that specializes in inexpensive Middle Eastern food, which in Portuguese is called *comida árabe* (Arabic food). Photo 6.8 shows Habib's cartoon mascot, a smiling caricature of a winking man with a large mustache and a red fez cap. We are old enough to remember that Frito Lay had a cartoon mascot named Frito Bandito, which was eliminated in the early 1970s because it supported an offensive stereotype of the Mexican bandit. Looking at the mascot of Habib's, it is evident that Brazilian sensitivities are not the same. These cartoon mascots and logo signs are another excellent example of passive nonverbal communication.

Another example of passive, nonverbal communication can be seen in the representation and symbols of trademarks and

6.9 The Brazilian Flag?
The Brazilian flag, modified for the colors of Belgium during the World Cup.

flags. For example, the Brazilian flag is filled with symbolism. The large green background represents the forests. The blue represents the ocean and sky. The yellow represents the wealth in gold. Each of the stars in the Southern Hemisphere's constellations represents the individual states, with the one star above the Ordem e Progresso (Order and Progress) banner representing the Federal Capital. Technically, it is considered desecration of the flag when it is altered in any way. However, photo 6.9 is one example of how the Brazilian flag was changed during the World Cup. In this photo, and there were many other similar versions from different countries, the colors of the Brazilian flag were changed to coincide with the national colors of Belgium.

HOW TO USE WHAT YOU KNOW ABOUT NONVERBAL SIGNALS TO ENCOURAGE GOOD COMMUNICATION

In general we believe that Brazilians are very accommodating to foreigners. This is helpful in the area of nonverbal communication because it means that they are understanding when foreigners do things differently. If a foreigner feels uncomfortable in a bikini and speedo, Brazilians may laugh about it a bit, but there is no problem in wearing what a person feels comfortable in. If a foreigner feels uncomfortable with physical hugs and kisses, again Brazilians do not push things on others. If you feel comfortable wearing a suit and tie, feel free to do so. Because of this, our first recommendation is to do what makes you feel comfortable. Given the mere fact that foreigners are different, they receive more understanding and leeway. There is no expectation that foreigners will or should act or be Brazilian.

At the same time, one of the challenges related to nonverbal communication is that so much of it goes on unnoticed. We generally do not know what we are communicating nonverbally. There may be times when miscommunications arise, and nobody will know the reason behind it. We remember a situation once where a Brazilian was with a North American. The Brazilian gestured by passing his thumb and index finger across his lips. He was trying to say that something was delicious. The American, however, interpreted the gesture to mean "zip up your lips." She was unsure why the Brazilian was telling her to be quiet. The Brazilian, then, caught on to her strange reaction, and as the two of them talked, they became aware of the miscommunication. Thus, our recommendation is to be flexible and forgiving. Pay close attention to how others react to you, and ask questions! Chances are that your first reactions and impressions will not always be accurate. But with close observation and open inquiry, over time the nonverbal cues will become easier to pick up on.

SUMMARY OF BRAZILIAN NONVERBAL COMMUNICATION

What we know about Brazil's nonverbal communication:

Kinesics
- The way people move their body, their gestures and their posture.
- Brazilians use a number of gestures that are not understood by North Americans: thumbs up, come here, snapping fingers, whatever, cheating, earlobe tug, hooking up, who knows, chin pat, talk to you later, phone, that is expensive, eyelid tug, no no, meeting over, betrayed by lover.

Affect display
- Relates to how much or how little a person displays an emotion. Do not confuse display of emotion with the intensity of the emotion.
- In general, Brazilians display emotions more openly than North Americans.

Oculesics
- Relates to how people use their eyes, such as eye contact, eye rolling, winking, and gazing.
- Be aware that Brazilian men will look at a woman with a longer gaze than what North Americans are accustomed to.

Dress and adornment
- Given the miles of coastal areas, Brazilians identify with beaches, and their dress often reflects this as well.
- Dress in professional settings.
- Both men and women are image and fashion conscious, and strive to have a "polished" look. Sophistication trumps casualness.
- Often, upper management has a more business casual style, and uniforms, coats, and ties are for those in service-oriented jobs.

Haptics and proxemics
- Haptics refers how people communicate through touch.
- Brazilians are likely to touch the person they are talking with, more than North Americans do.
- In professional settings, greeting with a handshake is fine. If one is a women, and the parties already know each other, a kiss on the cheek is also fine.
- Proxemics refers to how people use the space around them.
- Brazilians are likely to stand closer to the person with whom they are talking than North Americans do.

Passive nonverbal communication
- Those items that are less related to a person's body, and more about the environment around us.
- For example, we saw items such as the numbers of floors in a building, differences in handwriting styles, the symbolism of a national flag, and animated drawings that might seem inappropriate.

Communication strategies on how to deal with Brazil's nonverbal communication:

- If you feel uncomfortable in a bikini and speedo, Brazilians will understand. Wear what you feel comfortable wearing.
- Because we are often not even aware of our nonverbal communication errors, be flexible and forgiving. If something feels out of place, do not assume the worst.

7

BRAZILIAN
Temporal
Conception

Come On Over When You Can

How we think about time is what we call the temporal conception. We tend to think of time as something universal, but it really is not. Some aspects of time are personal. We have all had the experience of being involved in something so intensely that we seem to forget about time, and hours pass by without our even noticing it. We express this with clichés such as "time flies when you are having fun." In other ways, our concept of time is culturally constructed, and that is the focus of this chapter. Our approach closely follows the classic analysis of *monochronic* and *polychronic* time, as delineated nearly fifty years ago by Edward Hall. As such, we follow a similar approach in giving our examples regarding Brazil.

Monochronic time applies to those who coordinate their activities by doing one thing after another in sequence, which implies a need to schedule events with starting and ending times. This means that time is experienced as more rigid, and that activities are subordinate to the calendar. One supposed advantage of this is efficiency. That is to say, for example, that one can effectively measure the number of units that are produced every hour. Time that is governed by monochronic thinking may be less flexible, but it is often thought of as something that is tangible. Time can be lost, saved, gained, or squandered. Traditionally, North Americans are thought of as people who adhere to a more monochronic conception of time. As such, they are aware of their calendars, and they are sensitive to the importance of being on time. A Latin American executive once told us, "You Americans are amazing. You already know where you will be on October 5, at 3:00 pm in the afternoon. It's amazing." Indeed, an orientation toward monochronic time has both positive qualities and negative ramifications.

In polychronic cultures, conversely, multiple tasks can be handled at the same time, which implies that activities are subordinate to people, relationships, and the actual task. Because activities fuse together, there are not always beginning and ending times. Time is experienced as more fluid and flexible, and this entails more than simply "multitasking," because the focus is on making sure that people are taken care of. It is unreasonable to pin polychronic followers to specific deadlines because, after all, "things happen." Usually, Brazilian culture is thought of as leaning more toward polychronic time. And indeed, for Brazilians, time is more flexible. It is more difficult to separate personal time from work time. Break times and coffee breaks merge into general work time, and appointments are not locked into place.

Still, it is good to caution that we not overstate the effects of monochronic versus polychronic time. It is easy for North Americans to stereotype Brazilians in this regard, and vice versa. But for every example that you find, there is a counterexample. In fact, our recommendation is to consider the content of this chapter within the context of heuristic generalizations and not literal specifics. Especially as international connectivity grows closer and closer, an automobile factory line in Detroit might look similar to one in Curitiba, and a lazy afternoon of fishing in Paraná may resemble an afternoon of golf in Atlanta. When you find yourself feeling out of sync with international contacts, try considering whether their concept of time is monochronic or polychronic; but do not hold on to this as the only factor in how people manage their time.

Another point to keep in mind here is that differences in time conception probably are better seen on a sliding scale than as an either/or division. We touched on this in chapter 1. When Edward Hall first began describing these differences, he suggested that cultures *did* fall into either a polychronic or a monochronic group. So we repeat: Some cultures that are monochronic are actually stricter about adhering to schedules than others. The same can be said about polychronic cultures. There is a spectrum rather than fixed categories with firm definitions.

We have noted in other chapters that there are variations even within Brazil, and time conception is no different. We can see differences from region to region. The farther north you go in Brazil, the slower is the pace of life, the more lax people are about keeping to schedules, and the more strongly they rely on personal relationships and networks. Although we can safely say that regardless of region, Brazilians are polychronic in their time orientation when compared with those in the United States or Canada, it is equally safe to say that the people you meet in, for example, Macapá in the Far North will be more polychronic than those you meet in Porto Alegre in the Far South.

You can see this variation in the United States as well. Although the whole of the United States is correctly categorized as monochronic, you can safely expect that the farther into the Southeast you go, the slower is the pace of life, the laxer people usually are about keeping to schedules, and the more strongly they rely on personal relationships and networks. In other words, you can expect all people in the United States to be monochronic—and they are, when compared with Brazilians— but you can also safely expect people in Boston in the Northeast to be more monochronic than, say, those in Birmingham in the Deep South.

THE ENVIRONMENT AND TIME

The physical environment around us affects how we interact with time. In Manaus, for example, where the main transportation artery is the Amazon River, many buildings have boat docks instead of parking lots. As a result, in Manaus and the other towns and cities along the Amazon like it, schedules become subordinate to the time it takes for a boat to arrive at a given destination. On the coasts and at the beaches, many activities are subordinate to the times of high tides and low tides.

As the populations of Brazil's cities continue to explode, their roads and bridges can no longer accommodate the increasing number of cars. Traffic in São Paulo is some of the most congested in the world. In fact, on May 23, 2014—at the height of the World Cup events—São Paulo had a record 214-mile-long traffic jam! Even on a normal day, Paulistanos average traffic jams for more than 100 miles, with 2 hours of drive time commonplace (and even longer on Friday evenings, as people leave the city for recreation). São Paulo now holds the world record for number of private helicopters, because its business elites fly from helipad to helipad as a way to beat the traffic. The rest of us, however, expect delays to be inevitable, and often unpredictable. Not just in São Paulo but also in most of Brazil's large cities, there are simply more cars than what the roads have the capacity to handle.

There are simply hundreds of examples of how the physical environment affects the timing and scheduling of activities. Some places in Brazil have a rainy season and a dry season. This affects how and when people go from one place to another. There is even the fact that the closer one gets to the Equator, the more sunrise and sunset times vary less throughout the year. People need to adjust to sunsets at 5:15 pm when they are accustomed to having daylight until 9:00 pm. In other Brazilian cities, people walk more than they drive, and thus things just take more time. In those cities that are along the coast, the constant presence of a beach causes people to adjust time differently. They may, for example, take walks along the beach every morning, making early morning business meetings less likely. And those who work in agriculture, such as with sugarcane in São Paulo or grapes in Rio Grande do Sul, adjust their time to accommodate the planting or harvesting of their crops.

Our recommendation is that you not ignore the effects of the environment on how Brazilians divide their time, and thus that you relax about schedules. Those who insist on specific schedules will be seen as unreasonable, and in the end their insistence may not change anything anyway. Give the Brazilian environment the due consideration it deserves.

PERSONAL RELATIONSHIPS AND TIME

When we contrast Brazilian with North American temporal conceptions, we are actually comparing two seemingly unrelated things: adherence to schedules and personal relationships. It turns out that these two things are at opposite ends of the same line.

In figure 7.1, we have illustrated this as a seesaw, with a cartoon of people on one side and a clock on the other. The more we stress the importance of keeping to a schedule, the less we are able to build personal relationships. Conversely, the more we stress building personal ties with others, the less we can keep to a predetermined schedule. Thus, if you adhere to the clock, you cannot truly build personal relationships. And, in turn, if you

Figure 7.1
Adherence to Time, in Opposite Balance to Personal Relationships
Source: © Danielle Ryan. Used by permission.

place personal relationships first, you cannot really stick to a schedule.

It is important to keep in mind that our perceptions of scheduling and personal relationships are relative. In a monochronic culture such as the United States or Canada, people *think* they have a strong sense of personal relationships. Equally, Brazilians *think* they have a strong sense of time and scheduling. It is only when they find themselves outside their own cultural norms that they realize that these perceptions are relative.

The Seesaw Tipped to the Clock: The North American Perspective
To better understand this situation, it might help to explain North American and Canadian behavior. If you are from one of these countries, what follows should strike you as rather typical. We ask you to keep in mind, however, that from your Brazilian counterpart's point of view, this is all quite foreign.

In North America, you predetermine how long you will meet with another person. You keep a calendar and mark on it where you will be at what time. Although things sometimes go awry, on the whole, you probably do a good job with the things you are supposed to do and with the time you have allotted for doing them. This is especially true for work. From a North American perspective, if you run out of time, you simply schedule another time to meet. It seems normal to need to rush people out of your office, even before the task at hand is done, so that everyone can keep to their schedules. Unless there is a true emergency, it really does not matter how important or unimportant the issue at hand is. Likewise, your relationship with the other person makes no difference. In principle at least, if you are a North American, you will adhere to your schedule whether you are meeting with a customer for the first time or with your brother or sister, with whom you just happen to work. In fact, however, it is sometimes hard to cut off your time with a relative—which is one of the US and Canadian justifications for not hiring relatives. Similarly, we have heard many North Americans warn about getting too close to other people at work because it will begin to affect your impartiality (which, in US or Canadian terms, means showing no favoritism regarding the schedule). No matter the reason, in North America, you make a sharp distinction between personal time and work time.

If you are from North America, you might adhere to this sense of time most strongly in the workplace, but you will also find it affecting your appointments in all sorts of other settings. For example, you likely will think nothing of ending your lunch with a friend at a specific time so you will not be late for your next appointment—or just to set an ending time, even if you have nowhere else to go.

You probably do not think twice about any of this because everyone around you (i.e., all North Americans) sees this as quite normal. It almost never occurs to you that anyone would think that you are acting at all impersonally. In short, it may seem strange to think that Brazilians find all this to be strange and foreign.

The Seesaw Tipped to People: The Brazilian Perspective

If you are Brazilian, personal relationships generally trump adherence to the clock. The seesaw tips in the other direction. As a Brazilian, you may start each day thinking that you will basically keep to your schedule. That said, as a Brazilian, you know that every person you meet has individual needs and thus the time needed for each situation you face really depends on the person with whom you are dealing. Thus, from a Brazilian perspective, if you become involved in a complex situation with someone, you cannot just rush them out of your office. It is all right if you run a little overtime (or even a lot), depending on the situation. If the next two people on your schedule must wait a little, they will understand because they know that you would do the same for them (getting you even *more* off schedule).

In Brazil most people recognize that some matters are more important than others, and that we are not able always to predict their relative importance in advance. As a Brazilian, you also recognize that when you are dealing with someone you do not know well, it takes more time to figure out what they are really saying (i.e., building context, as we discuss in chapter 4). In any case, as a Brazilian you recognize that people who know each other well can trust one another, and that this familiarity will speed things up. As a result, every Brazilian knows that it is much harder to predict how long a first meeting with a new customer will take than it would be to predict how long it will take to answer a quick question from a brother or sister who happens to work at your company. The same may be true for North Americans, of course—but again, here we are discussing relative cultural emphases.

In Brazil, the better you know someone, the less likely it will be for you to ask him or her to leave, because in the end your friendship or family relationship is more important than getting home at a specific time. Because of this, as a Brazilian, you do not make that great a distinction between personal time and work time. From a Brazilian perspective, if you are building relationships the right way at work, then your work relationships will blur into your personal relationships. For Brazilians, all this comes as second nature as long as they stay in Brazil. It is hard for most Brazilians to grasp fully how foreign—and frustrating—this can be for most North Americans.

The main point here is that whether you do all these things from a North American point of view or from a Brazilian one, you probably do not think twice about any of this. As long as you stay within your own culture, your way seems normal. It may even seem strange to you to think that people *could* do things another way. If you are a North American, it may never occur to you that you are acting at all impersonally or that, from a Brazilian perspective, you have a very weak sense of personal ties. If you are a Brazilian, it may never occur to you that you are at all unusual in how you handle your schedule and that, from a US or Canadian perspective, you have a very weak sense of time.

TEMPORAL CONCEPTIONS IN PERSPECTIVE

It is important to remember that neither the North American nor the Brazilian conception of time is right or wrong. They are just different. How you view this is simply a matter of your own cultural perspective. Both conceptions work quite well. But there is at least one exception in each culture where the other temporal conception is in force—and these exceptions can be useful in explaining each culture's conception to members of the other culture. In Brazil, monochronic time is very much the norm at the airport. In the United States and Canada, polychronic time is the norm at the doctor's office.

Brazilian Airport Time: A Monochronic Exception

Brazilians adhere to flight timetables fairly strictly. Admittedly, once a flight has been delayed or canceled, the situation is handled in a typically Brazilian, polychronic manner. The comparison is close enough to North American monochronic time that most Brazilians will understand the parallel because any Brazilian who has been to the airport will have experienced airport time. This makes it useful as an analogy for the common North American temporal conception.

The US and Canadian Doctor's Office: A Polychronic Exception

The analogy we like to use to explain Brazilian polychronic time to North Americans is the doctor's office. The world over, doctors' offices run on polychronic time, even in the United States and Canada. Let us look at a typical doctor's office visit in some detail.

The Sign-In

The first thing you do when you go to a doctor's office is sign in with the receptionist. This sign-in takes place in virtually every doctor's office in the world. The receptionist acts as the doctor's scheduler. How is this like what happens in Brazil? Unlike in most situations in North America, the receptionist is able to bend the schedule. If you do not have an appointment but you have an urgent need, the receptionist can squeeze you in. If you are a friend or relative of the receptionist, you can also get squeezed into an otherwise overbooked schedule. In Brazil, the schedule bends on a case-by-case basis, depending on the specifics of a situation and on how well you know the people involved.

The Waiting Room

After signing in, you sit down in a waiting room. What better evidence could there be that you are in a polychronic setting where the schedule will be flexible than that you are given a place to wait? How is this like what happens in Brazil? Schedules are approximate, not exact. Even North Americans accept this situation because they know that the doctor may need more time for emergencies or unexpected reactions.

The Examination Room

After waiting in the big waiting room, next, a doctor's assistant leads you *to one of several* examination rooms. Thus, the doctor is seeing several patients at the same time. This is the definition of polychronic: doing multiple things simultaneously. While the doctor has assistants gather information (to provide contexting), he or she goes from room to room seeing patients in each of the many rooms. How is this like what happens in Brazil? Brazilians handle multiple tasks simultaneously.

Personalization during the Doctor's Visit

When the doctor does see you, he or she will almost always pepper your examination with a conversation. Some of this is to put you at ease, to build trust. And some of this is to gather relevant information about your condition. The timing of this is difficult to schedule well, particularly if the doctor has never seen you. You may find that the subject you came in to discuss may not actually be what is most important. You may have thought you were going to see the doctor about indigestion, for instance, and the doctor notices an irregular patch that might be skin cancer. The doctor must then treat not only the relatively minor heartburn but the unexpected and much more serious possibility of cancer. How is this like what happens in Brazil? Situations develop organically rather than according to a preset schedule. In a typical North American, monochronic approach, there would not be enough time to address both the scheduled reason for the meeting (the heartburn) and the more important but unscheduled reason for the meeting (the possible cancer). In a North American office setting, you would need to schedule another meeting to discuss the second issue. Even in North America, doctors do not do this, however; they finish the task at hand, even though it extends beyond the time that was scheduled for you. The point here is that though doctors are the exception in the United States and Canada in acting like this, in Brazil almost all schedules are handled in this "doctor-style." That said, in most situations, the Brazilian temporal conception does not work well in North America, and vice versa. They are simply so opposite from one another that they clash.

EMBRACING THE POSITIVE: AT THE YACHT CLUB IN RIO DE JANEIRO'S BOTAFOGO BAY

It is easy to see the negative side of what you are used to experiencing. If you are from Brazil and you are working in or visiting the United States or Canada, nobody seems to care about anybody else with any real depth. If you are from North America in Brazil, nobody seems to be able to do anything on time. Either way, this can feel deeply frustrating. That said, there are positives as well, and you should try to embrace these.

One of the positive results of being in a culture that follows polychronic time, like Brazil, is that activities become more flexible. Activities are subordinate to people, not clocks. We recall an experience a number of years ago in Rio de Janeiro, when we were accompanying a group of North Americans who were involved in negotiations with a Brazilian group. We had a full agenda, and meetings were scheduled with a number of people all day long. The meetings were held at a location in beachfront Leblón, one of Rio's most affluent neighborhoods. At lunchtime, one of the Brazilian hosts was driving us to a nearby restaurant, also in Leblón, no more than five minutes away. En route to the restaurant, our host found out that one of the Americans in the group liked sailboats. Instantly, she suggested that it would be better to have lunch at the Yacht Club in Botafogo Bay. It would be a little out of the way, 30 minutes or so, but lunch there would be more enjoyable. She then called her secretary to cancel the lunch reservation at the nearby restaurant and to make a new reservation at the Yacht Club. Indeed, we had a delightful lunch at the Yacht Club, including fantastic views of Sugarloaf Mountain.

Just about the time that lunch was ending, our host mentioned that in nearby Flamengo Bay there was a temporary exposition of racing sailboats that were racing around the world and just happened to be in Rio. She suggested that we make a brief stop to see the sailboats. After an interesting visit and walk around the sailboats, we finally started heading back to resume our meetings in Leblón, which by this time were almost 2 hours behind schedule. On the way back to Leblón, our host called the home offices, explained that "traffic" was slow, and asked to please reschedule all our afternoon appointments. Even though our lunch and afternoon activities had been pleasant, it was easy to see why the Americans of the group had become rather anxious. Their full schedule had already been tight, and now it would be even more difficult for them to complete all their work. We are happy to say that in the end, we did see everyone scheduled for that day. Little adjustments were made here and there; and by the end of the day, we had taken care of all the meetings.

We have reflected on this story many times. In fact, what if the story had unfolded in, for example, Detroit? Chances are, the story would have taken a different turn: "Mr. Olivares, I wish we had known that you like sailing. We could have had our lunch at the Yacht Club. Too bad; but next time you are in town, we will have to take you to the Yacht Club." In other words, in Brazil we were able to modify the agenda and take advantage of the Yacht Club and the exposition of racing sailboats. In Detroit we probably would have lamented not being able to do so, because other things were already scheduled. That experience taught us the positive effects of being in a culture that has a more flexible way of looking at time and schedules. In Rio we actually took advantage of the moment to change the lunch's location; in Detroit we probably would have lamented not being able to do so. Over the years, we have seen countless similar examples. Brazilians are adept at being flexible with their time and schedules. From a North American perspective, things seem to be less organized and structured; but at the end of the day, things work out.

The world experienced a similar issue vis-à-vis the 2014 World Cup. Before the World Cup, there was much media focus on the slow progress of infrastructure projects. People were worried:

The stadiums were not going to be ready, the Fédération Internationale de Football Association was frustrated with construction projects, the airports would not be able to handle the increased traffic, hotels were not prepared, and so on. The whole world was trying to force Brazil to follow their specific schedules, but Brazilians were simply following their internal polychronic clocks. In the end, things went fairly smoothly, but not without causing the world to hold its collective breath in hopes that there would not be any disasters.

Our recommendation is that you take advantage of a Brazilian's ability to be flexible. This is more than the proverbial ability to "stop and smell the roses." Brazilians are adept at quickly reacting to new parameters. We recall the years of hyperinflation in Brazil. With 30 percent inflation each month, Brazilians were forced to become adept at making quick changes. They learned to hedge funds, make short-term investments, and find creative ways to not lose their money. There is still a sense of this among Brazilians today. In an environment where things change quickly, long-term planning gives way to short-term modifications. As a result, Brazilian strategies are extremely creative, which you can use to your advantage.

GOING OUT TO DINNER IN BRAZIL

Recently, a group of about twenty Brazilian executives was in Austin for several weeks of training. We took them to experience Texas barbeque at Austin's Salt Lick, one of the area's most famous barbeque restaurants. The Brazilians, we are sure, have pleasant memories of the brisket, ribs, and sausage, but what stuck out most in their minds was the sign posted at the restaurant's entrance, which reads "To satisfy all BBQ lovers, we appreciate your dining time be limited to 1.5 hrs."

The visiting Brazilians could not believe this sign—which actually informs customers that they have a limited time to dine! Never mind how long the line of customers might be; this would never happen in Brazil. People can stay at a restaurant for as long as they like. Perhaps these North Americans were thinking that

7.1 The Saltlick BBQ
To satisfy all BBQ lovers, we appreciate your dining time be limited to 1.5 hrs.

a lot more money can be made if more customers move through the restaurant more quickly. A Brazilian's reaction would be that maximizing the dining experience of the few is more important than making profits from many. In polychronic cultures, the schedule is subordinate to people's relationships.

When Brazilians go out to a restaurant, it is important to understand that this is often the main activity. They are not going out first to dinner and then to somewhere else. Dinner is the activity. When Brazilians go out to dinner, they may spend hours at the restaurant. After being seated, it is not unheard of to sit and chat for 30 minutes or more before they even look at the menu. Drinks, appetizers, the meal, dessert, coffee—all these take time. There is no reason to rush through any of these parts of the dinner. Brazil does in fact have fast food restaurants, and most of the modern shopping malls there have a food court. However, the general tendency, even at small corner restaurants, is to slow down. If someone orders fresh pineapple juice, plan on watching the cooks cut up the pineapple, chop it in a blender, pass it through a sieve, and then finish it off with sugar added in the blender again. Do not be surprised, if a given food requires an herb, when you witness the cook walk over to a plant, cut off a few leaves of the herb, and then go prepare the dish. Brazilians simply enjoy dinner at a restaurant at a different speed. In the end, when the bill is asked for, again do not be surprised if it takes 10 to 15 minutes to arrive. And after dinner is paid for, feel free to remain at the restaurant for as long as you like.

What monochronic thinkers define as "efficiency" polychronic thinkers may interpret as a lack of emotion and feeling.

If the reason we go out to dinner is to be with friends, from a Brazilian perspective, why would we limit this experience to seconds that click away on a stopwatch? When you are in Brazil, we recommend that you enjoy the pace. There is no doubt that some days, those with a monochronic time perspective will feel like they are being less efficient in their time management. But look at the meaning behind what feels like a "waste of time." If the inefficiency is related to interpersonal relationships, ignore it. If the inefficiency is related to non–people issues, feel free to work on ways to improve the situation.

PARTIES AND SOCIAL EVENTS

There is a huge difference in how Brazilians approach work-related schedules versus social events. Especially in large cities like São Paulo, professional appointments follow tight schedules. Of course, if someone is running late, courtesy demands a phone call to explain the reason behind the delay. However, in general, professional meetings and scheduled events begin more or less on time.

However, in the case of social events and parties, forget the calendar, forget the clock, and forget worrying about being on time. Social events are a completely different matter. The author who is a Texas resident recalls a time when some Brazilian friends invited him to a birthday party for their twin sons. The party was scheduled for 12 noon. Upon arriving at 2 pm, he was still the first guest to arrive! When the Brazilian host family teased him about coming early, his only response was that he had tried. He had come 2 hours after the appointed time! Our recommendation is that if you are invited to a social event, try to attend with other Brazilians who will pick you up. That way, you can wait at home for them to pick you up, and you will arrive at the same time as the others.

An aspect of North American social events that totally baffles Brazilians is when they see invitations for a party with both starting and ending times. In the United States it is not uncommon to receive an invitation that says, for example, the party will be "next Saturday, from 3:30 pm to 6:00 pm." A Brazilian will react with shock. "Perhaps you can tell me when a party begins, that I understand. But how can you tell me when a party ends?" Yet, indeed, in monochronic cultures, the activity is subordinate to its scheduled time period. So even if everyone is still having a great time, if something is scheduled to end at 6 pm, chances are that it will end then. But Brazilians simply cannot understand why a person would stop doing what all are enjoying, simply because the clock tells you that it is time to move on to something else.

Years ago, the University of Texas won the national championship in football. The university announced that a celebration would take place at the special events center near campus. At the scheduled time, the players and the coach appeared on the stage. They made a few remarks, the band played the school song, and everyone cheered madly on cue. When the event ended, everyone stopped cheering and returned to their vehicles to go back home. When you stop and think about this event with a temporal conception in mind, it represented an extremely weird manipulation of emotions, whereby the cheering and celebration were subordinate to the schedule. This is not to say that North Americans do not take to the streets to spontaneously celebrate sporting events. By comparison, however, when Brazilians take to the streets after a soccer victory, fans dance in the streets, strangers hug one another, and everyone spends the night celebrating with no thought of the clock. The sensation is very different.

Another example of the subordination of emotions to a schedule can be seen when Americans attend sporting events. They may be cheering with passion and emotion, and then there is a TV timeout. For the next 5 to 7 minutes, everyone in the crowd waits for the game action to resume; and when it does, everyone goes back to cheering loudly. Americans can even compartmentalize their emotions so that they become subordinate to the clock! Brazilian soccer is very different because the clock never stops and the fans are free to sing, chant, and carry on all game long. There is no pause for a TV timeout, and indeed it would be extremely bizarre to have one.

In sum, Brazilians do not understand how parties and social events can have both starting and ending times. It is important to note that Brazilians do not arrive late at social events because they have no respect for other people. And it is not because they are lazy about time. It is more that for them, the event should be subordinate to the person, and not vice versa. People are more important than schedules.

PRECISE SCHEDULING

Recently, a group of Brazilians was traveling in the United States, and we asked them what cultural differences they noticed between Brazil and the United States. Their answer was public bus schedules. They are impressed with these schedules because they give precise times. In Brazil people may say that a certain bus will come by every 15 or 20 minutes, but they will never say that a bus will come by at, for example, 12:48 pm. Indeed, the following photograph shows one of the public bus routes in Washington, where the departure times vary throughout the day

G2
P Street-LeDroit Park Line

▶ Westbound To Georgetown University
Monday thru Friday —
Lunes a viernes

Route Number	#301 Bryant St. NW (Howard University)	3rd St. & Rhode Island Ave. NW	P St. & New Jersey Ave. NW	P & 14th Sts. NW	P & 20th Sts. NW (Dupont Circle) [M]	37th & O Sts. NW (GEORGE-TOWN UNIVER-SITY)
AM Service — Servicio matutino						
G2	5:10	5:13	5:16	5:21	5:26	5:35
G2	5:35	5:38	5:42	5:49	5:56	6:06
G2	6:00	6:03	6:07	6:14	6:21	6:31
G2	6:25	6:28	6:32	6:40	6:48	7:00
G2	6:45	6:48	6:52	7:00	7:08	7:20
G2	7:02	7:05	7:09	7:18	7:27	7:40
G2	7:15	7:18	7:22	7:31	7:40	7:53
G2	7:27	7:30	7:34	7:43	7:52	8:05
G2	7:40	7:43	7:47	7:56	8:05	8:18
G2	7:52	7:56	8:00	8:11	8:21	8:35
G2	8:05	8:09	8:13	8:24	8:34	8:48
G2	8:17	8:21	8:25	8:36	8:46	9:00
G2	8:32	8:36	8:40	8:51	9:01	9:15

▶ Eastbound To Howard University
Monday thru Friday —
Lunes a viernes

Route Number	37th & O Sts. NW (George-town University)	P & 20th Sts. NW (Dupont Circle) [M]	P & 14TH STS. NW	P St. & New Jersey Ave. NW	3rd St. & Rhode Island Ave. NW	#301 Bryant St. NW (HOWARD UNIVER-SITY)
AM Service — Servicio matutino						
G2	5:45	5:56	6:02	6:08	6:12	6:17
G2	6:15	6:26	6:32	6:38	6:42	6:47
G2	6:38	6:49	6:55	7:01	7:05	7:10
G2	7:05	7:17	7:23	7:30	7:34	7:40
G2	7:25	7:37	7:43	7:50	7:54	8:00
G2	7:46	7:58	8:06	8:14	8:18	8:24
G2	7:59	8:11	8:19	8:27	8:31	8:37
G2	8:11	8:23	8:31	8:39	8:43	8:49
G2	8:24	8:36	8:44	8:52	8:56	9:02
G2/	8:40	8:52	9:00	-	-	-
G2	8:55	9:07	9:15	9:23	9:27	9:33
G2/	9:10	9:22	9:30	-	-	-
G2	9:25	9:37	9:45	9:53	9:57	10:03

7.2 US Public Bus Schedules
A North American bus schedule with precise times.

and precise times are given. This is common in monochronic cultures, but would be almost laughable in a polychronic culture.

HOW TO USE WHAT YOU KNOW ABOUT TIME
TO ENCOURAGE GOOD COMMUNICATION

The recommendations that we offer here come with an initial caution: It is easy for people who have more of a monochronic way of looking at time to believe their way is superior to that of those who follow more of a polychronic way. Yet, as with other cultural tendencies, there are strengths and weaknesses on both sides. It is not the foreigner's job to try to turn Brazil into a more monochronic society; and indeed any effort to do so would be inappropriate and ineffective. This may be obvious; but especially in professional settings, companies do send expatriates to Brazil to work at local subsidiaries or branches. As part of such an assignment, there is a fine line between teaching employees to effectively improve quality and misunderstanding the valid reasons why Brazilians do things a certain way. Foreign visitors and expatriates rarely understand how local residents work with suppliers, factory workers, union representatives, government agencies, and police forces. When it comes to time parameters, allow the locals to take the lead.

Our recommendation is that you resist thinking that time and schedules are not important in Latin America. Simply because we have talked about the flexibility of time among Brazilians, one cannot assume that time and schedules do not matter. You will find, especially in large cities like São Paulo and Rio de Janeiro, that professional appointments are carried out according to tight schedules, with beginning and ending times for meetings that are followed with precision. Similarly, do not make the mistake of thinking that somehow people are "more lazy" in polychronic cultures. You will find that Brazilians work hard, long hours, and that many even enroll in evening courses in addition to their work schedules. We have encountered North Americans who misinterpret a polychronic time conception as laziness, and nothing could be further from the truth.

Finally, observe how Brazilians view coffee breaks. From a North American perspective, it sometimes feels as if Brazilians are constantly taking long breaks. Their devotion to a little *cafezinho* with biscuits or cookies approaches ceremonial proportions; and to be honest, these are important times for interacting with colleagues and coworkers. We have discussed the importance that Brazilians put on building context and developing relationships. A coffee break is not just a time to rest from work; it is also a time to interact with others. If someone invites you to *tomar um cafezinho* (have a cup of Brazilian-style coffee), this is really an opportunity to interact. Accept the invitation, and then expect to spend the next half hour building ties with those with whom you are working. And for the coffee drinkers: Once you get used to the strength of *cafezinho*, you will never want to go back.

SUMMARY OF THE BRAZILIAN TEMPORAL CONCEPTION

What we know about Brazil's notion of time:

Monochronic time
- Those who coordinate activities by doing one thing at a time.
- Things are scheduled, and schedules are adhered to.
- Activities are subordinate to the schedule.
- Enhances the ability to measure the number of units per hour.
- Time can be lost, saved, gained, or squandered.
- North Americans follow, in general, monochronic time.

Polychronic time
- Multiple tasks can be handled at the same time.
- There are not always clear beginning and ending times for activities.
- The use of time is more flexible, and the clock is subordinate to the activity.
- Brazilians follow, in general, polychronic time.

Environment and time
- Brazil's physical environment affects how people react to time.
- Transportation subordinate to the river in the Amazon.
- Traffic subordinate to available roads and bridges in cities like São Paulo and Rio de Janeiro.

Schedule versus personal relationships
- Temporal conception is really more of a balance between time given to the clock and time given to people.

- In North America the clock mandates how long we spend with people.
- In Brazil, relationships with people mandate how we manipulate the clock.

Yacht Club in Botafogo
- Changing lunch to the yacht club was an unplanned adjustment to the schedule; flexibility is key.
- In a monochronic culture, such as North America, we would have lamented not being able to make the change, because plans had already been made.
- Brazilians are adept at reacting quickly to new parameters.

Dining in Brazil
- A Brazilian restaurant would never limit how long customers can sit at their table.
- Efficiency is subordinate to taking care of people's emotions and feelings.

Parties and social events
- Professional events in Brazil basically begin and end as scheduled.
- Social events in Brazil almost always begin late, and there is no way to say when they will end.

Communication strategies on how to deal with Brazil's notion of time:

- Be cautious about thinking that somehow monochronic time is superior to polychronic time. Both have advantages and disadvantages.
- Do not suppose that Brazilians have no respect for time and schedules. Especially in large cities like São Paulo and Rio de Janeiro, you will find that professional appointments adhere to tight schedules.
- Coffee breaks are common in work settings, and they are extremely social and interactive times to be with other colleagues.

Case Study

Sitting Secure in Latin America, Brazilian Style

Now that we have seen the application of the LESCANT approach to Brazilian business communication, in this chapter we present a brief vignette—a cultural case study—that provides a chance to apply what we have learned to the scenario of a real situation in Brazil. The names of the company, the location, and the people involved have been changed, but the events actually occurred as reported in this vignette. The case deals with a United States–based multinational security systems company, which we call ABC Security Systems, that is trying to balance how much to impose uniform standards on all its worldwide subsidiaries with how much to allow for local modifications. Carolina Battipaglia, the company's Latin American marketing director, is the person assigned to deal with both the local representatives and management from the home office. The case focuses on her precarious position.

After the case itself, we then provide the observations and opinions from three Brazilian and three US executives who have experience working in similar situations. These comments represent their actual opinions, and these are the real names of these people, who have graciously offered to share their opinions. We also add a few of our own comments and observations about the case.

After reading the facts of the case and the opinions of the expert executives, you will then find a final section with questions and topics to help you assess the cultural issues about this case and come up with your own solutions. To sum up the case preliminaries:

> *Company:* ABC Security Systems
>
> *Focus:* The manager of the Latin American Marketing Division, who must coordinate worldwide operations on one hand and specific Brazilian differences on the other hand.
>
> *Cultural conflict:* Often, North Americans assume that all countries of Latin America are alike, ignoring the cultural differences that exist among the various countries of Latin America.

INTRODUCTION AND SYNOPSIS

Carolina Battipaglia oversees the Latin American Marketing Division of the multinational ABC Security Systems. Her position has created an opportunity for her to appreciate this firm's operations from two distinct perspectives. Sometimes, she spends her time working with the people at the corporate home office in San Jose, California. Other days, she dedicates her time working with all the various marketing managers throughout Latin America. It is a common mistake for people to think of Latin America as a homogenous group of countries. In reality, each country (and indeed, each region within a large, varied country like Brazil) exhibits dramatic differences from the others. This is one of Carolina's two major challenges. Her second big challenge is that ABC Security Systems' Latin American division represents only a small percentage of its total volume of business, so she must manage a larger number of projects with a smaller number of workers. Together, these two factors create specific problems for her.

This case exemplifies some of the issues related to how people from different cultures react to hierarchy. Carolina notes that in North America, relationships are "flat." People there thus seem to give a lot of importance to the idea that everyone is equal and that power and authority are shared and exchanged. But in Latin America, and indeed in most of the world, people must finesse themselves around vertical positions. In this story, Carolina provides a relevant example: She is able to report data directly to the home office in the United States; but in Latin America, before sharing the data with others generally, she feels a need to go through all the various levels of hierarchy within the region's offices.

In the vignette we are exposed to the Brazilian term *jeitinho brasileiro*, which Denise Coronha Lima defines as "the creative ways that Brazilians deal with challenging situations." Indeed, no discussion of Brazilian style would be complete without an introduction to *jeitinho*—which, of course, chapter 5 above considers in detail. Many Brazilians almost demonstrate a sense of pride in their ability to finesse and finagle things to help them get their way.

In this case we also see that Carolina laments the need to "hold people's hands" and to need to repeat things over and over again in multiple meetings. The comments from the Brazilian executive Wagner Palmiere provide a nice description about why this is so, explaining how Brazilians need to rely on friendships to develop trust. Many times, extra meetings and confirmations are necessary to put people at ease, especially in the absence of solid, trusting relationships.

CASE SCENARIO

Imagine being in the business of providing security systems for homes and small businesses in São Paulo, which is not exactly known as a safe haven from crime. One can almost hear the advertising: "If we can provide security in São Paulo, we can do it in your town too." For Carolina Battipaglia, this is precisely what she does on a daily basis. She oversees the Latin American Marketing Division of ABC Security Systems, a multinational company with operations worldwide. And the company is truly multinational. Although its home office is located in San Jose, California, its current president is from Malaysia and its former president was from England. Its Brazilian manager is actually from Chile, and its sales and development manager in Brazil is from Colombia. Its vice president for marketing is from the United States, and the lead accountant in its São Paulo local office is from the Netherlands. Although the company is global in scope, Latin America represents only 9 percent of its total worldwide operations. As a result, though its North American, Asian, and European divisions are well developed and well staffed, its Latin American divisions are less developed, and their staffs are spread thin.

Carolina is from São Paulo. (In fact, you may have noticed her Italian family name. At the turn of the century, nearly 1 million Italian immigrants arrived in Brazil, and almost all settled in the State of São Paulo. See chapter 3 above for more on immigration.) Carolina has worked in the São Paulo office, located near Avenida Paulista, for the past four years. Previously, she worked in the marketing division of a local television station. At ABC Security Systems, she oversees marketing for all of Latin America, which in the south includes projects in Brazil, Argentina, and Chile, and in the north includes Mexico, Puerto Rico, and Colombia. The majority of her effort and time is spent looking at strategic plans, where to focus their efforts, which projects should be identical throughout all of Latin America, and how projects should differ from one region to another. These logistics can be challenging. Part of this implies that Carolina spends much of her time reporting back to the home office about progress in her region. Conversely, she must deal with marketing issues among the several countries in Latin America, which are all culturally diverse. "We are very fragmented here in Latin America," she confesses, "and almost all of the other worldwide regions have an infrastructure that allows them to implement procedures without some of the challenges that we have in Latin America." Interestingly, she is the first to admit that in many ways, it is easier for her to communicate with the home office than to bring together all the various Latin Americans. She remembers once, during a Web seminar with the home office, that the participants were assigning who would be in charge of the various projects that were being proposed. In every other region, a different person was assigned to each project. For Latin America, however, Carolina was assigned to all the projects. After a while, the other people in the seminar were asking "How many projects does Carolina direct?" It is just one of the realities of overseeing one of the company's minority regions. All the other regional groups would say something like "Let's do XYZ . . ."; but in Latin America, Carolina just did not have the manpower to assign these projects to different people.

With respect to her work with the Americans at the home office, Carolina is quick to note that it is generally easy to work with Americans. "They are very good at human relations, and they work at all levels of the hierarchy." She believes that relationships among North Americans are more "flat"; that is to say, you do not need to worry about people in the United States and Canada asking "Why did you go over my head?" Carolina believes that in Brazil, and really in all of Latin America, you must be more sensitive to hierarchies. "People here in Brazil are more 'vertical.' They put more effort into playing their roles," she says. She finds herself, to use an American baseball term, "covering her bases" more with the Latin Americans. Rather than just implementing a decision, in Latin America she makes sure that she has first talked with everyone—and in the right order. For example, ABC recently compiled research comparing the effectiveness of online marketing among the different countries in Latin America. When Carolina presented the results to the home office, she simply presented the data. However, before she publicly presented the same results to her Latin American colleagues, she was more careful to show a "draft" of the presentation to the various regional managers. "I just wanted to be more careful about the vertical repercussions of making sure that I didn't step on any toes." In her view, this extra step is not as necessary with the North Americans because they are less focused on level, power, and authority issues.

Similarly, Carolina feels that Americans are adept at being transparent. Of course, relationships and networking are important, but she finds the Americans to be very open and honest. "In Brazil you find yourself always thinking, 'What are they not telling me?' or 'What is really going on here?'" She thinks that in Latin America, there is an initial resistance to things because people are not as open in their communication. "I always know where the Americans stand; they are brutally honest sometimes," she adds. In Brazil, people like to say that the Brazilians are really good at free style, improvising, and being flexible. Maybe so, but Carolina also believes that behind this *jeitinho brasileiro* lurk their unspoken hidden agendas. "I almost prefer to deal with the North Americans' openness and frankness. There is less guesswork with the Americans," she adds.

Conversely, Carolina admits that sometimes the Americans put work above logic. She remembers one time, for example, when the company brought in people from all over the world for a series of face-to-face meetings in San Jose. "We had all traveled all night, from all parts of the world, and they wanted to start 10 hours worth of meetings at 8:30 am!" Nobody was able to perform well in the meetings. Everyone was half asleep, with hardly any feedback and almost no interaction. However, Carolina adds, "To their credit, I will say that after that experience, the company made a new rule: No more post-travel Monday morning meetings!"

Another challenge that Carolina has with the Americans is related to holiday and vacation times. "Normally, I cannot take my vacation during regular Brazilian vacation times because the home office in the United States cannot relate to our vacations in February." In the United States, everything closes up for the Christmas season, but Carolina knows that by January 5 everyone is back to work full force. "It's one thing for me to work in February," observes Carolina, "but what the Americans cannot understand is that it is almost impossible for us to do market research during that time. Almost anyone who is part of our target audience is on vacation, and this isn't just true for Brazil, but it happens in all of Latin America." Add to this the fact that ABC Security Systems' fiscal year begins in October. This means that Carolina must juggle the US holidays in December and June with the Latin American holidays in February, and coordinate all this with the fiscal year that begins in October: "October is kind of crazy here."

In some ways, Carolina's biggest challenge comes more from her work in dealing with the local Brazilians and the other Latin American regions. She confesses that in Brazil, people are really adept at making you feel good: "You leave a meeting and you think that you've made great progress." The problem is that they just do not always follow up on what they say they will do, and as a result, Carolina admits to doing a lot more "hand holding" with the Brazilians. She also believes that Latin Americans seem to want to hold more follow-up meetings, to talk about previous meetings: "It drives me crazy! Why don't we just make a decision in the first meeting?" But no, the tendency is to have long initial meetings that end with no resolution and then have follow-up meetings to start all over again.

Carolina also observes that you cannot put all the Latin Americans into one big basket. "The Mexicans, for example, have a passive resistance to everything," she says. "All the other Latin Americans identify with being Latin American. Even the Chileans, Argentines, and Brazilians, despite their various animosities, consider themselves to be Latin American brothers—but not the Mexicans. They are Mexican, and everyone else is a foreigner." She says that the Mexicans may say, "yes" to things, but in the end they do it their way. For example, last year it was decided that, globally, the ABC Security Systems website needed to have a consistent look and feel. Everyone had to modify the way that the various national sites looked. This included the use of graphics, the number of illustrations, and the links about home security systems. When the final sites were launched, although the Mexican team had agreed to everything, in the end they used different graphic representations. "Our homes don't look like the ones in the corporate graphics," they complained.

To provide another example, Carolina explains that in Brazil, security and safety are less focused on home security systems (which become the responsibility of the apartment complex where they are installed) and more on protection from street crimes. In São Paulo there is a greater fear of being robbed in traffic than there is of being robbed at home. Consequently, things such as bulletproof windows and even armored cars come into play much more than in other locations. Conversely, Chileans, for example, are much less worried about street crimes, and their focus tends to center on home burglaries in the summer months (December–February), when many are away from home on vacation.

Finally, Carolina has an anecdote to share about crime in Brazil. Recently, she heard from an American friend who was traveling with his wife in Rio de Janeiro. They were resting on a park bench, when suddenly a guy appeared who tried to distract them while a second person attempted to steal their bags from behind. The American, who speaks Portuguese fairly well, yelled something at the would-be thieves. In response, the thieves said, "Oh, I'm sorry, I thought you were Americans. I didn't mean to take anything away from you. Are you here from São Paulo? What do you think of Rio?" So it looks as if Carolina has discovered a new security measure: Learn to speak a little Portuguese, and act like you come from São Paulo!

OBSERVATIONS AND COMMENTS
FROM AMERICAN EXPERTS

Christine Uber Grosse, Chief Executive,
SeaHarp Learning Solutions
I would like to focus on the differences in communication style among Brazil, Mexico, and the United States in this case. Carolina Battipaglia expresses her frustration in dealing with her Mexican counterparts. She complains that their "yes" does not really mean "yes." She needs to realize that Mexicans value courtesy and politeness in business communication. For them, it would be extremely rude to disagree openly with her. Instead, they prefer to say "yes" and then do what they need to do, even if it is different from what they have said. "Yes" gives them room

to maneuver, and keeps the door open for further negotiations. It also gives them leeway to do what they have said—or the opposite. The important thing for Carolina to remember is that Mexicans place a high value on courtesy and indirectness. It would be unthinkably rude to say no so directly.

Not only does "yes" not mean "yes" in Mexico and other collectivist countries; "maybe" often means "no." For example, to openly say "no" to an invitation is considered rude. In many cultures, including Mexico, people assume that "maybe" probably means "no." To illustrate, if Consuelo invites you to her party, and you say that maybe you can attend, she will understand that you probably do not intend to come. She will not be offended, but understand that you are being polite, rather than simply saying "no." That would be too harsh and direct, as well as rude.

Carolina further contrasts US transparency and directness with Brazilian indirectness. She goes against her own culture by preferring the US style in a business context. Brazilians, as well as Mexicans, are comfortable being indirect. Mexican managers have told me on numerous occasions that they consider too much directness to be offensive and rude. They would rather go around a topic delicately, and discuss it indirectly for the sake of courtesy. Latin American business communication style clearly favors indirectness.

My recommendation for follow-up: Rather than resenting the lack of transparency in Latin business communication, Carolina can try to appreciate the courtesy, finesse, and polish of Latin American indirectness. Rather than suspect an ulterior motive or hidden agenda, she can understand that Latin Americans are trying to be courteous. She will also realize that Latin Americans may consider US business communication style rather offensive and lacking in finesse. They may find it far too direct, brash, and rude.

Mary Risner, Associate Director, Center for Latin American Studies at the University of Florida
This case touches upon several enigmas about Latin America that makes it such a fascinating region to study or work with. Carolina's dilemma over the lack of homogeneity throughout

Latin America is a challenging one. Those unfamiliar with the region may make assumptions of cultural similarity due to the fact that the majority of countries speak Spanish when many were actually dominated by other European colonial powers at some point in history, and may also be different due to indigenous cultures or African slave populations brought in that have influenced social infrastructures and local economies. Firms wishing to do business in any world region may want to consult country profiles readily available online through respected sources such as *The Economist* and the BBC's Web pages, which will provide some background and save a potential loss in profits due to intercultural misunderstandings. While there are some common cultural threads throughout Latin America, it is best not to assume that everyone is the same because most Latin Americans are very proud of their unique national culture.

The significance of hierarchy is extremely embedded in Latin American culture, even beyond an individual's workplace. I was surprised when Mexican colleagues I was working with in a volunteer nonprofit organization were unwilling to approach another Mexican of a higher professional ranking than they to address problems with a project. It seemed like such a reasonable thing to do where this individual was not their boss, but an equal in the volunteer context. However, they understood the unofficial lines of power and were not willing to suffer consequences of stepping out of their "place," even in the broader system.

I can also relate to Carolina's quandary on how to read Brazilians, when on one hand they seem so friendly and flexible, yet on the other hand it is tough to perceive what they are really thinking. However, these mixed signals are what make navigating Brazilian culture so intriguing. I believe a couple of things are happening here. First, Brazilians tend to want to please and avoid confrontation, especially with foreigners visiting Brazil. As part of this effort to "please," Brazilians will use a variety of subtle tactics to avoid directly saying no by not responding or stalling. Additionally, in my experience working within the university environment, it just takes time to build a relationship with Brazilians for them to finally give you the whole story and the politics behind a problematic scenario. An interesting read on this topic is a book titled *Communicating with Brazilians: When "Yes" Means "No."*

I am not sure if the indirectness of Brazilians also leads to misunderstandings about timely follow-up in Brazil, but it definitely seems to be a big problem, even among Brazilians themselves. Over the years I have had several business colleagues send a note thanking me for fulfilling a simple task, saying that it is so uncommon among their compatriots!

Stephen Kaufmann, Founder and Chief Executive of LingQ.com
I believe that it is hard to have one set of rules for one group of people and another set for another group. It is best to develop a working style that takes elements from many cultures, and then to make minor adjustments depending on each situation. Otherwise, we risk coming across as not genuine. There is no doubt, for example, that it makes sense to do behind-the-scenes work before a meeting, in order to make sure that various "stakeholders," or meeting participants, are familiar with your point of view before a meeting. It is often not realistic to come to a meeting with a "brilliant" PowerPoint presentation and hope to bowl everyone over. It is possible to get some form of agreement in this way; but if there is not solid support, the implementation can suffer. The practice of lobbying for support ahead of time, as Carolina has to do in South America, is a good habit to develop. By the same token, follow-up is also key, regardless of where we work. I prefer not to make assumptions about people based on national stereotypes. If some people are less cooperative, or tend not to carry out their commitments, then I will have to deal with it. It is best to assume that it will be necessary to follow up, regardless of the nationality of the people with whom we are dealing. While North Americans are less hierarchical and appear more easygoing, it is never amiss to flatter their sense of importance by respecting hierarchies. So this is also something we can learn from other cultures. It is important, in my view, to be sensitive to the individual differences among the people we deal with but to try to resist ascribing national stereotypes to these differences. It is even more important not to assume that

"our way" is right simply because we are American, Canadian, Brazilian, and so on, or because "we have always done it this way."

We need to be flexible and respectful of the people we deal with. This includes respecting their holiday schedules, if we want to do business in their environment. In my experience, there is always some degree of cultural defensiveness behind the scenes, when we work across language and cultural divides. That is why it is important to find time for socializing, so that people can learn to like and respect each other for who they are, and to feel respected for who they are. This will go a long way to minimizing the national or cultural defensiveness that can spoil the atmosphere in international enterprises. I also believe that we need to deal with people as individuals and avoid cultural stereotypes. Mr. Gomez wants to be accepted as Mr. Gomez, and not as a stereotyped representative of all Mexicans. In Japan I have seen fluent Japanese speakers, fully in tune with Japanese culture, who were unsuccessful at business because they were more interested in flaunting their "Japanese skills" rather than listening to their business partners. I have seen people who spoke no Japanese and yet were successful because they were good judges of people, and were also capable and reliable in their business activities. However, those people who can combine good language and cultural skills with good business and interpersonal skills are usually the most successful of all.

OBSERVATIONS AND COMMENTS
FROM BRAZILIAN EXPERTS

Denise Coronha Lima, Founder of Rio Total Consultancy
For my comments, I would like to talk with Carolina Battipaglia, and this is what I would say:

DENISE: Like you, Carolina, I also know these two worlds very well; Americans always focus on the task in hand while we, Latin Americans, only seem to be concerned about people.

CAROLINA: Sometimes, Denise, what San Jose expects from us just seems so unrealistic.

D: Just as Americans ignore differences within Latin America, very few Latin Americans really understand the American way of doing business. But none of that is new. What is really bothering you?

C: After four years, I ask myself how I could make these two worlds talk with each other. And how ABC could actually take advantage of the diversity.

D: Well, now we are going beyond logistical issues and thinking about creating links between people. Is that what you mean? I wonder if some kind of global conversation would help increase the company's international operations.

C: That would be possible. Selling residential security systems in São Paulo reminds me of the story of the two shoe factories that sent representatives to India to search for new business opportunities. When they returned, the first person recommended that they forget about selling in India because nobody wore shoes. The second person, however, reported that a gigantic country of shoeless people would have to be, without any doubt, a priority market. So the fact that Brazil and Chile are still so far behind in security technologies, would that represent a commercial barrier or a tremendous opportunity?

D: Good question. Who could help answer it?

C: All of our Latin staff, they could help. And everyone in San Jose could, too.

D: Well, Carolina, what if you had get-togethers and let everyone share their visions and goals? Most important, find out where they can and cannot be flexible. It is not about who has the best PowerPoint presentation; it is about honest face-to-face communication. Ask the right questions and listen carefully. By bringing together the Puerto Ricans, the Americans, the Argentines, and everyone else, it will mean that you all share the same information about the various markets in which you operate. Also, you could find out what they understand by respect, hierarchy, and feedback so that you can all speak the same language. As a result of all this, ABC may actually be a multinational company where, for sure, everyone collaborates to add value and increase profitability.

c: I could have a lot more rapport with everyone.

d: Yes, and they would respond with creativity. You will find out that you are not alone and could even delegate some of the workload you get from California. With communication that is more open and with more meaningful relationships, you will be on the right path to get beyond the 9 percent international operations.

c: What about the Mexicans? I have been thinking about them.

d: Listen, passing judgment on any other culture is a trap. Why do the Mexicans want to stand out? We are just dealing with the tip of the iceberg here. With *jeitinho* (the creative ways that Brazilians use to deal with challenging situations), you will be able to find out what is beneath it that is so important to them.

c: From this angle, it feels simpler.

d: Simple is good.

Gleverton Munno, Senior Manager of External
Relations for Dell's Global Operations Team

As to ABC's Latin American divisions being less developed than in other regions, this is a typical situation. Latin America is increasingly important, high-growth, high-opportunity markets, but it is still not as relevant in terms of total revenue or total operations. The international nature of ABC's team in Brazil seems to be something unrealistic to me. In the real world, doing business in Brazil is extremely complex. It demands experienced professionals who know about Brazil, its language, its markets, and its people. It sounds like ABC may need more Brazilians on the regional team if they really hope to do things properly in South America. For example, do you know how much time the average company spends on tax procedures in Brazil just to invoice customers and process/pay taxes to the government? Believe it or not, it is 2,600 hours a year. Compare that with the 250 hours a year that it takes in the United States. This may vary from one industry to another, but typically, Brazil, Argentina, and Colombia make up 80 percent of the total market share in South America. So Brazil for sure, and maybe Argentina and Colombia, should be given specific attention and dedicated teams. Probably the other countries could be treated as a single bulk, as the rest of Latin America.

As to the vertical repercussions and making sure that Carolina did not step on any toes, that is true. However, this may also shift from country to country. It also depends on whether you work for a truly global company or not. In some companies there is a corporate culture that does not change as much from one place to another. I agree that the less globalized companies may face situations that are more like the one reported in this case scenario. One of the most interesting cultural aspects of working with Brazilians is the fact that they do not know how to say no. This is because they work to maximize relationships, even more than being honest or simply objective. The ability to interpret what people want to say instead of what they really say is one of the most important skills that an American can develop while interacting with Brazilian colleagues. Finally, I thought it was interesting that the Americans learned not to have Monday morning travel meetings. Being sensitive and flexible is something that is related to good management and communication practices. I am not even sure that this is necessarily a cultural issue. I believe it is more an issue of taking time to put yourself in the other's shoes and try to see how others feel.

Wagner Palmiere, Senior Manager of US Central Region, Mexico, and Central America, Ascendant Technology
I think this scenario describes fairly well the reality of someone who works for an American company in a Latin American context, specifically Brazil in this case. Considering my experience as a Brazilian who works with Americans, even I agree that it is much easier to communicate with Americans than with Brazilians (and I believe this is so, even taking into account the absence of a language barrier). The Americans are more honest, direct, and truthful when handling business. You do not need to worry as much about the "hidden" intentions and motives that are more part of what happens when you are dealing with Brazilians. When you work with Brazilians, one of the primary reasons that you need to strengthen a relationship is to be able to trust what a person tells you. Maybe that is the reason why we

Brazilians, and I think this is generally true of people throughout Latin America, seem to value follow-up and review meetings, as described in the case. We love to reassess matters and discuss them over and over again before making a decision. Due to issues related to a lack of trust, we try to get some kind of guarantee; we want to be completely comfortable and secure that we will not be misled or deceived. The bottom line is that generally Brazilians are very nice people to work with, but we are very suspicious too. As is mentioned in the case, I also agree with the idea that Brazilians tend to be more vertical and vigilant of "covering their bases." Again, I believe this is related to our general lack of trust. My sense is that Americans are more solution driven than Brazilians, who are more sensitive about hierarchies. In my experience this behavior is also aggravated whenever the Brazilian economy is not doing so well. The fear of losing your job makes people more guarded and cautious. Given the different sizes of the American and the Brazilian economies, this is probably even more of a reality in Brazil specifically, and in Latin America generally. Another consequence of this distinct economical reality is resource overstretch. In Brazil the tendency within a company is to pile up roles and responsibilities on one specific employee, similar to the example that Carolina mentioned during the Web seminar. Constraints and limitations in new job offers result in less flexibility for employees as they look to move or change jobs. Actually, this is similar to what we saw happening within the American workplace during the last few years of the recession.

My recommendation for someone who interacts and does business with Brazilians is to invest time in building up good friendships and relationships. One of my former bosses once told me that at the end of each and every project with a customer, our goal is always to be able to take him or her out for a "*chopp*" (draft beer).

OBSERVATIONS AND COMMENTS FROM THE AUTHORS

Wagner Palmiere concludes his comments about this case with the observation that the end "goal" of every project is to be able to meet at a bar for a social drink. (Brazilians also joke that this *chopp* needs to be *estupidamente gelada*—stupidly cold!) It is, of course, too simplistic to say that North Americans just focus on the task and Latin Americans focus on people. However, Wagner's point is well taken: The end goal is not simply to conclude the business but also to conclude the business by celebrating with people. Almost all the guest executives, both those from the United States and those from Brazil, included comments about the increased importance of relationships and people among Latin Americans.

Given the focus on people, it is not surprising that Brazilians are more cautious about the words that they use with others. In the case study, Carolina specifically mentions that things that she just openly states among the North Americans in the home office are repeated in Latin America with more care and with greater deference to the people involved. Indeed, when dealing with Brazilians, there is a level of guesswork and of wondering what people are not saying. All this is centered on a conscious effort to avoid confrontation on a personal level. Gleverton Munno goes so far as to say that the most important skill that North Americans can develop is to interpret what Brazilians want to say, as opposed to what they really say. It is no wonder, then, that North Americans—especially those from the United States—are perceived as being brutally blunt, because they come out and say things so much more directly. Readers will also note that Wagner expressed his comments by bringing up the issue of trust. For North Americans, trust is built into the system. They trust their laws, their policies, and their procedures. Brazilians, conversely, put their efforts into finding people they can trust. Consequently, our authors' recommendation is, when dealing with people, especially people from different cultural backgrounds, that we respect their preferences to be people focused or task focused. Similarly, this is what Denise Coronha is trying to express in her advice to Carolina. Listen to others and respect their opinions, because it is always beneficial to appreciate another person's perspective.

Second, and possibly the most important aspect of this case, we read that Carolina believes that North Americans have a tendency to lump all Latin Americans into the same category. It is easy to think that, culturally, Mexico, Peru, and Argentina are all the same, because after all, people have placed them in the same category: Spanish-speaking countries that are located south of the United States. In an effort to manage and summarize things, it is natural to sort data into specific categories. The problem comes when we rigidly think of these categories as inflexible realities. The example from the case study is quite illustrative. All of ABC's national branches were modifying their websites to have a similar look and feel worldwide. This, however, simply did not work for all the regions. The Mexican group, for example, did not want to show houses on their site that did not look like houses in Mexico. ABC Security Systems can choose to be frustrated at their nonconformity; or it can benefit from a new perspective (coincidentally, one with which other Mexicans will identify when buying a security system). This is not a trivial matter. In the case, Carolina provides three specific examples to show how security concerns differ regionally (i.e., single-family homes in the United States, car safety in Brazil, and empty homes during vacation seasons in Chile). Similar differences will also exist beyond the world of security systems. Munno notes that doing business in Brazil is extremely complex and that experienced professionals need to know about its language, markets, and people. The same is true for all the other regions. Our recommendation is the same. Even when planning marketing and sales strategies in the United States, people almost never lump all of North America into one category. The same applies to Brazil, Mexico, and Argentina, and it applies even more if we are using some vague category like "Latin America."

Finally, a word about holidays and vacation times, and how they differ from one part of the world to another. Here, our recommendation comes from the experience in being in Argentina during the soccer games for the America's Cup, in Brazil during Carnaval, in China during New Year's, and in Europe during the August summer vacation weeks. It is essential that North Americans recognize and respect the importance of holidays, vacations, and other similar local customs. Imagine what the repercussions would be if, in the United States, we expected work to be totally unaffected by Independence Day, Thanksgiving, Christmas, and Super Bowl Sunday. In the case vignette, we learn that Carolina herself was even willing to work on the days during local holidays, in order to communicate with the home office. However, what the home office was unable to resolve was the fact that Carolina could not work with anybody locally on those days. The company could impose its will on Carolina, but not on the local community.

For those readers who want to discuss these issues further, consider the following topics and questions for discussion:

1. We hear that the ABC Security Systems is truly international, but we also see that its Latin American division is less developed. Does this tell us more about the company or more about the situation in Latin America? In terms of the LESCANT approach, what does this tell us about social organization?

2. People seem to lump all of Latin America together as one unified geographic location. Mary Risner offers some reasons why. What are the ramifications of such a division? Christine Uber Grosse's comments focus on specific differences between Mexican and Brazilian tendencies. How do you react to these observations? Where does this fit in the LESCANT approach?

3. Christine Uber Grosse recommends that rather than resent Latin Americans' lack of transparency, we should appreciate the courtesy, finesse, and polish of Latin American indirectness. Think of specific instances when this can come into play. If you think of this in terms of Brazilian *jeitinho*, how does that change your perspective?

4. Both Mary Risner, as an American, and Wagner Palmiere, as a Brazilian, say that it is hard to get beyond the Brazilians' pleasantness to get at what they are really thinking. How does one go about doing this? How does this relate to the LESCANT category of nonverbal communication?

5. Stephen Kaufmann suggests that even though North Americans are less hierarchical, it is "never amiss to flatter

their sense of importance by respecting hierarchies." What are the pros and cons of this recommendation?

6. When Denise Coronha Lima provides Carolina with advice, she includes the observation that it is important to find out where people can be flexible and where they cannot. In what ways will this come into play in the case of ABC Security Systems? In thinking about the LESCANT approach, in what ways are Denise's comments extremely "Brazilian"?

7. Gleverton Munno suggests that Brazilians do not know how to say "no." Consequently, the ability to interpret what people mean, instead of what they say, becomes an important skill. Do you agree? And if so, how does someone acquire this skill?

8. Suppose you understand the importance of Wagner Palmiere's suggestion that you take time to build up friendships and relationships with Brazilians, but your superiors in the home office back in the United States do not see its value. What can you do? How would their understanding and acceptance of the LESCANT approach affect your ability to present this argument?

NOTES

CHAPTER 1

1. US Central Intelligence Agency, *The World Factbook*, www.cia.gov /library/publications/the-world-factbook/geos/br.html.
2. Education First, "Brazil," www.ef.edu/epi/regions/latin-america /brazil/.

CHAPTER 2

1. For the population densities of cities, see City Mayors Statistics, "The Largest Cities in the World by Land Area, Population and Density," http://citymayors.com/statistics/largest-cities-density-125 .html.
2. Instituto Brasileiro de Geografia e Estatística, "As 200 cidades mais populosas do Brasil," August 28, 2014, http://exame.abril.com.br /brasil/noticias/as-200-cidades-mais-populosas-do-brasil.
3. For data on the world's major cities, see Eurostat, "City Statistics Illustrated," http://ec.europa.eu/eurostat/cache/RSI/#?vis=city .statistics&lang=en; and City Mayors Statistics, "Europe's Largest Cities," www.citymayors.com/features/euro_cities1.html.
4. For basic statistics—e.g., GDP and GDP per capita—see International Monetary Fund, "IMF Data," www.imf.org/external/data .htm.
5. *The Economist*, "Special Report on Brazil: The Road to Hell," September 28, 2013, www.economist.com/news/special-report/21586680 -getting-brazil-moving-again-will-need-lots-private-investment-and -know-how-road.
6. For data on roads and highways, see the US Central Intelligence Agency, *The World Factbook*, "Field Listing: Roadways," www.cia.gov /library/publications/the-world-factbook/fields/2085.html.
7. Simone Palma, trans., "São Paulo Had the Worst Traffic Jam in History," *Folha de São Paulo*, November 15, 2013, http://www1.folha .uol.com.br/internacional/en/saopaulo/2013/11/1371995-sao-paulo -had-the-worst-traffic-jam-in-history.shtml.
8. For data on the use of energy, see US Energy Information Administration, "Brazil's Key Energy Statistics," October 9, 2015, www.eia .gov/beta/international/country.cfm?iso=BRA.

CHAPTER 3

1. For data on gross domestic product per capita, see the World Bank database, http://data.worldbank.org/indicator/NY.GDP.PCAP.CD.
2. For cost-of-living comparisons between Brazil and the United States, see Numbeo, www.numbeo.com/cost-of-living/compare _countries_result.jsp?country1=Brazil&country2=United+States.
3. For data on world poverty, see the World Bank database, "Poverty & Equity," http://povertydata.worldbank.org/poverty/country/BRA.
4. The Brazilian government provides excellent information through the Secretaria de Assuntos Estratégicos, www.sae.gov.br.
5. Mikaela Conley, "Nips/Tuck Nations: 7 Countries with Most Cosmetic Surgery," ABC News, April 25, 2012, http://abcnews.go.com /Health/niptuck-nations-countries-cosmetic-surgery/story?id= 16205231.
6. See, e.g., S. D. J. Pena, L. Bastos-Rodrigues, J. R. Pimenta, and S. P. Bydlowski, "DNA Tests Probe the Genomic Ancestry of Brazilians," *Brazilian Journal of Medical and Biological Research* 42, no. 10 (October 2009), www.scielo.br/scielo.php?pid=S0100 -879X2009005000026&script=sci_arttext#Abstract.
7. See "Regiões onde se estabeleceram," *Imigração Italiana* blog, May 1, 2011, http://migriitaliana.blogspot.com/2011/05/regioes -onde-se-estabelecera.html.
8. "Brazil's Changing Religious Landscape," Pew-Templeton Global Religious Futures Project, July 18, 2013, www.pewforum.org/2013 /07/18/brazils-changing-religious-landscape/.

CHAPTER 4

1. Edward T. Hall, *The Silent Language* (Garden City, NY: Doubleday, 1959).

CHAPTER 5

1. For data on the time required to start a business, see World Bank, "Data: Time Required to Start a Business (Days)," http://data .worldbank.org/indicator/IC.REG.DURS.
2. For data on doing business by country, see the World Bank's Doing Business website, "Economy Rankings," www.doingbusiness.org /rankings.
3. Transparency International, "Corruption Perceptions Index 2013," www.transparency.org/cpi2013/results.
4. Anderson Antunes, "The Cost of Corruption in Brazil Could Be Up to $53 Billion Just This Year Alone," *Forbes*, November 28, 2013, www.forbes.com/sites/andersonantunes/2013/11/28/the-cost-of -corruption-in-brazil-could-be-up-to-53-billion-just-this-year-alone/.
5. "Após 5 meses, roubo de vigas de Perimetral, no Rio, ainda é mistério," *Globo*, October 3, 2014, http://g1.globo.com/rio-de-janeiro /noticia/2014/03/apos-5-meses-roubo-de-vigas-da-perimetral-no -rio-ainda-e-misterio.html.

6. Derick W. Brinkerhoff and Arthur A. Goldsmith, *Clientelism, Patri-monialism, and Democratic Governance: An Overview and Framework for Assessment and Programming* (Bethesda, MD: Abt Associates for US Agency for International Development, 2002), http://pdf.usaid .gov/pdf_docs/Pnacr426.pdf.

7. "Obituary: Eduardo Campos," *The Economist*, August 6, 2014, www.economist.com/news/obituary/21612167-eduardo-campos -brazilian-politician-and-presidential-candidate-died-august-13th -aged.

8. Robert P. Kaufman, "The Patron–Client Concept and Macro-Politics: Prospects and Problem," *Comparative Studies in Society and History* 16 (1974): 284–308.

9. Robert Gay, "Rethinking Clientelism: Demands, Discourses and Practices in Contemporary Brazil," Digital Commons @ Connecti-cut College, January 1, 1998, http://digitalcommons.conncoll.edu /cgi/viewcontent.cgi?article=1002&context=sociologyfacpub.

CHAPTER 6

1. Lydia R. Pozzato, "Interpreting Nonverbal Communication for Use in Determining Deception," *Forensic Examiner* 19, issue 3 (Fall 2010), www.biomedsearch.com/article/Interpreting-nonverbal -communication-use-in/241273588.html.

2. Sérgio Rebêlo and Natália Borelli, "Analysis of the Brazilian Deodor-ant and Antiperspirant Market," Factor de Solução, 2006, www .factordesolucao.com.br/pdf/Deodorants-Antiperspirants-Brazil .pdf.

speakers of Portuguese, 4–5; nonverbal communication and, 153–54; pronouns, 15, 123; reasons for, 84–86, *84–86*; rule orientation and, 77–79; slowing down and speaking simply, 14; social organization and, 70–73, *71–72*; strategies for, 90–95; subtlety of, 17, 75, *87–88*, *87–89*, *90*; temporal conception and, 174–75; understanding, 80–81; variations in, 81–82, 83*t*; written vs. oral communication, 14. *See also* conversations; gestures; nonverbal communication and behavior; Portuguese phrases and terms

conversations: compliments and, 5, 56–57; flirtation and, 56, 139, 145; greetings and, 146–48, *147*; proxemics and, 148–49; sports and, 68–70; touch during, 149–50

"cool" slang expression, 130–31

Corinthians soccer team, 68

coronelismo (clientelism), 110–15, *116*

corporate culture: collectivism and, 64–66; contexting, 82, 91–95; *coronelismo* (clientelism) and, 110–15, *116*; energy use and, 38; hierarchies in business relationships, 179, 181–82, 187, 191–92; laws and authority and, 104–6; meetings and, 135, 183, 187, 191–92; nepotism and, 49–50, 113; professional attire and, 140–44; professionalism and, 54–55, 82, 95, 146–47; purchasing behavior of Brazilians, 54; sexism and, 54–57; sexual harassment and, xvii–xviii, 55–56, 138, 145–46; temporal conception and, 174–75. *See also* authority and power; case study

corruption, 50, 103–4, 106–7, 109

cost of living, 52

credit cards, 34, 41

crime, 32–34, *33*, 41–42, 183–84. *See also* theft

cronyism, 111–12

cross-cultural communications. *See* context and contexting; LESCANT approach; *specific languages*

cultural norms. *See* context and contexting

cultures: crafting a universally adaptable style for variances among, 188; diversity among, 194–95; ethnic origins of Brazilians and, 60–61, *61f*; misunderstandings, 186–87. *See also* ethnicity and race of Brazilians; social organization

Curitiba, 7, 34, 35

customer service, 55, 72

dams, 38

dating, 133

Daylight Savings Time, 22–23

deadlines, 158

delivery services, 9–10

dining out, 10–11, 34, 169–71, *170*

disabled persons, 47, *47*–48, *49*, 71, *71*

discovery of Brazil, 2

discussion topics, 195–96

doctor's office visits, 165–67

Domestic Maids Law, 120–21

domestic workers or maids, 120–21, *121*

dress and adornment, 139–45, *140–41*; business casual, 143; company representation and, 55; men's professional dress, 142–43; women's professional dress, 143–44

driving. *See* automobiles; transportation

droughts, 38

smoking, 85, *86*, 117–18, *118*
soccer, 68–70, *69*, 103, 172. *See also* World Cup (2014)
social cues. *See* context and contexting; corporate culture
social events, 171–73
social organization, xvii–xviii, 45–74; class system, 51–54, 53*f*; collectivism and, *63–65*, 63–66; communication strategies and, 70–73, *71–72*; compliments to opposite gender, 56–57; education, 50–51; ethnic origin of Brazilians, 60–62, 61*f*; family connections and professional services, 49–50; gender roles, 54–56; kinship and family values, 46–49, *46–49*; race, 57–60, 59*f*; religion, 66–68, *67*; sports, 68–70, *69*
Spanish heritage, 60, 61*f*
Spanish language, 3–4
sports: leisure time activities, 68; Olympics (2016), 103, 107; soccer, 68–70, *69*, 103, 172; World Cup (2014), 103–4, 107–8, 153, *153*, 168–69
Standard Time, 22–23
stereotypes, 187–88
street art, 36, *36*
strikes, 108–9, *109*
subtlety, 17, 75, *87–88*, 87–89, 90, 186
sugarcane, 24, 37–38
summer, 34
supermarkets. *See* shopping and customer service

taxes, 105–6, 190
taxis, 41, 70, *71*, 137
temporal conception, xx, 157–76; communication strategies for, 174–75; dining out and, 169–71, *170*; late arrival and, 171; parties and social events, 171–73; personal relationships and, 161–64, 161*f*; in perspective,

164–67; physical environment and, 159–61; positive aspect of, 167–69; precise scheduling and, *173*, 173–74
Teresina, 70, *71*
theft, 40–42; from automobiles, 183–84; gesture for, 132; steel beams for road construction, 106; tourism and, 184
"thumbs up" gesture, 130–31
time. *See* temporal conception
time zones, 22–23
titles and names, 123–25
topography of Brazil, 22–24, 23*f*
touching, 145–50, *147*, *150*
tourism: dining out, 10–11, 34, 169–71, *170*; English language use, 7; hotels and tourist sites, 37; shopping and, 48–49, *49*, 52, 72; theft and, 184. *See also* beaches; transportation
trade, xv–xvi, 5–7, 24
trademarks, 152–53, *153*
traffic. *See* automobiles
trains, 30–31
transparency in business relationships, 182
Transparency International, 106
transportation: boats, 159–60; buses, 71, *71*, 173–74; rail lines, 30–31; roads, xvii, 29–32, *30–32*, 30–32*f*; safety and, 40–42, 183–84; taxis, 41, 70, *71*, 137. *See also* automobiles
Treaty of Tordesillas (1494), 2
trust, 50, 191–93
"tsk" sound, 135

Uber Grosse, Christine, 184–85
UNESCO World Heritage Site, 35
uniforms, 55
United States: Brazilian students at universities in, xvi; Latin America, assumptions about, 193–94; trade with Brazil, xv
United States, compared to Brazil, xxi–xxii; authority and law, 122; collectivism, 63–64,

66; communication, 184, 193; compliments on appearance in business settings, 56–57; consumerism, 54; corruption index ranking, 106; cost of living, 52; crime and safety issues, 32–33; dress and personal appearance, 139, 141–44; ease of starting business, 105; education, 50–51; gestures, 130–34; haptics and proxemics, 145–49; hierarchies in business relationships, 179, 181–82; holidays, 182, 194–95; hydropower, 38; income levels and middle class, 52; kinship and family, 46; language use, 4–5, 8–9; nepotism, 49–50; openness and frankness in business, 182; per capita income, 29; population density, 25–26; public health announcements, 117–18; sexism, 56–57; sexual harassment, xvii–xviii, 55–56, 138; size, 22, 23*f*; sports, 69; temporal conception, 159, 162, 165, 171–73. *See also* low-context cultures; North America, compared to Brazil

universities, 50–51, 145

urban population, 25–27, 26–27*f*
Uruguay, 52, 106

vacation time, 182–83, 194–95
values, 70–72, 71
Veloso, Caetano, 39
Venezuela: corruption index ranking, 106; ease of starting business in, 105
vulgar gestures, 131, 135

weather and seasons, 23, 34, 143–44
winter, 34
women: clothing and personal grooming, 141–45; comfort level with body shapes, 140, *141*; compliments from men, 56–57; femininity, 54–55; gazing at men, 138–39; gender roles, 54–56; proxemics, 148–49; saying hello and goodbye to, 146–48, *147*; sexual harassment of, xvii–xviii, 55–56, 138, 145–46
World Bank's Doing Business project, 105
World Cup (2014), 12, 103–4, 107–8, 153, *153*, 168–69
World Factbook (CIA), 2, 29
World Heritage Sites, 35

Orlando R. Kelm, PhD, is an associate professor of Hispanic linguistics at the University of Texas at Austin, where he teaches courses in Portuguese and Spanish, focusing mainly on business language and the cultural aspects of international business communication. He also serves as the associate director of business language education at the University of Texas at Austin's Center for International Business Education and Research. His research and publications center on the cultural aspects of international business and the pedagogical applications of innovative technologies in language learning, focusing mainly on Latin America and Brazil.

David A. Victor, PhD, is a tenured professor of management and international business at Eastern Michigan University, as well as a consultant, author, and editor. He teaches courses on managing world business communication, international management, and international business and offers a series of seminars on doing business in various countries, including Brazil. As a consultant, he has run training programs and coached leaders for more than two hundred companies and organizations, from global 500 companies to governments and nongovernmental organizations. Among his many publications was the groundbreaking *International Business Communication* (HarperCollins, 1992), which introduced the LESCANT Model used as the framework for this book.